BEYOND THE FEED

The Social Media Success Formula

ZOE CAIRNS

www.beyondthefeed.com

Beyond The Feed

First published in 2023

Mabel and Stanley Publishing Info

Cover design: Goce Veleski

Editing and Publishing: Karen Stanley | Mabel and Stanley Publishing

DEDICATION

"I dedicate this book to my Nan, Janet Bevan who we sadly lost this year, and who had written many books and poems that were published. Nan, you have given me the inspiration and determination to get this book written, and to you I am grateful. I love and miss you but know you would be proud."

CONTENTS

FOREWORD

"I know that the book will be filled with the same expertise and passion for her job as she has shown for the last decade - I think you simply cannot go wrong ...".

by Franky Saegerman, Head of Digital Insights, NATO

Throughout my career and more specifically in my roles as NATO's Head of Social Media (2012-2016) and NATO's Head of Digital Insights (2016-2019) I have encountered a broad and diverse range of social media experts - or some of them 'so-called experts'. As with everybody, during our careers most of these people come and go but some of them leave a 'permanent mark' and will always make you think back to that first time you heard them present.

Zoe Cairns is one of these people who stands out from the crowd. Back in 2015 I invited Zoe to be the keynote speaker at NATO's Social Media Forum for International Organisation in Montenegro. Although the scene was not very mainstream and the audience not your traditional social media users who are interested in 'for-profit' tips and tricks, her keynote grabbed the audience's attention from the first sentence and kept them engaged throughout the presentation.

At the time, as the owner and CEO of ZC Social Media, Zoe had already positioned herself as an expert in both content creation as well as analysis and assessment of the then lead social media channels and during her keynote in Montenegro I personally got to witness the ease with which she was able to transfer her knowledge and expertise to the audience. In the years that followed she also provided Social Media Training at the NATO School in Oberammergau.

We have kept in touch over all these years, and I have seen Zoe's interactions grow from events and trainings to local communes/cities, where I had the privilege to keynote at one of these events in Kent, to being the 'go to person' when BBC wants to have a TV presenter who knows her stuff. Each time she provides clear and common-sense advice but at the same time she also keeps up-to-date with the quickly and ever-changing world of social media, from new platforms to algorithm changes, to what works and what does not work on all these platforms.

Zoe is also a kind person who willingly shares her knowledge and expertise and sometimes does this even pro bono through free online trainings or seminars.

When Zoe informed me about her book - which was nearing completion - and asked me to write the foreword, I did not hesitate for a second. I know that the book will be filled with the same expertise and passion for her job as she has shown for the last decade - I think you simply cannot go wrong ...

FRANKY SAEGERMAN

HEAD OF DIGITAL INSIGHTS NATO

https://www.linkedin.com/in/frankysaegerman/

Chapter One

My Why: The Story Behind the Pages

There was a time when I wasn't known as a social media consultant, and it is that time that I think back to now, and what prompted me to write this book. I also recently lost my dear nan who had written quite a few books throughout her life and having always wanted to write myself, I thought it was time to carry on her legacy!

So... here it goes. Let me tell you about how I got to my first day as a social media person! I say person, as I dislike the word expert! In my opinion, an expert is someone who knows everything there is to know about their chosen field, and I surely couldn't know every single thing about the digital world, as it's always updating.

Anyway, in my previous role I was an IFA/Mortgage broker specialising in helping property investors to build their property portfolios. I loved it, right up until 2008 when we started to see the market change. A recession had begun to hit, and it was then that my boss at the time told me I had to start generating my own leads.

The thought of networking and doing a 60 second pitch was daunting, but I knew that in order to build my profile and reputation, I had to push myself, get out there, and get to know more people in the local area.

My good friend also told me about Facebook, it had literally only just launched and was mainly for college students in the US, but here in the UK, we had a news feed; all I could see when scrolling through was people out enjoying themselves, or people in fancy dress outfits. I questioned, "How am I going to use this professionally?"

At the top of the Facebook feed was a search bar, and in the search bar I typed who my target audience were - 'property investors' - and all these groups appeared, full of property investors. I thought, "Wow, there is my target audience." I had been travelling to Manchester, Leeds, Berkshire, and London to get in front of all these potential clients, and here they were engaging in these groups.

I joined 10 groups and started to introduce myself in them. I must admit, I did get approached by a few administrators of the groups telling me to stop posting and spamming the group! This made me sit back and start to listen to the conversations in the group. You will notice further in this book, I talk about whether you are a broadcaster or an engager and, in this situation, I was a broadcaster; I needed to take a step back to be an engager.

By taking a step back and listening to the conversations going on in the group, I was able to relate on a more personal level to the group members. One day, I noticed a conversation from a property investor looking to purchase a property above a launderette. I instantly knew I could assist. I went into the group and clicked on the comment box under the post and typed, "I can help you with this. I'm unable to give advice online but feel free when convenient to call me."

What happened next, was my first success from social media. The property investor called. I was able to assist with a mortgage lender and complete a deal. The property investor was so impressed with my help that he posted a comment back in the group telling others how I had helped him, along with a rating for my service.

This engagement led to me building my reputation and presence in the group for further conversations, enquiries, and clients. Before I knew it, I had many property professionals in estate agencies, other mortgage brokers and property finders, reaching out for me to help them with the lead generation process using social media. It was then I decided that it was time for me to think about branching off on my own.

In 2010, that's exactly what I did. To be exact, the 10th of February 2010. Not the best time to leave the company I was working for, but now I look back and think, was there ever a good time?

I remember that feeling of leaving. At first, I felt great,

"The world is my oyster!"

By Monday morning, I got up and cried, thinking about what I had done; how I was going to pay the mortgage?

I went from being an IFA/Mortgage broker on the Friday to being a Social Media Consultant on the Monday. Who would take me seriously? Especially, if people asked, how long I had been doing this for!

However, I threw myself into my new role. I networked 'as a social media consultant'. I did every networking event you could think of, I saturated Kent, making sure I got to know local businesses, entrepreneurs, local brands, and other social media enthusiasts. The more I networked, the more consistent I was online, and the more people became familiar with my name and brand. And that's how Zoe Cairns Social Media was formed.

I would love to share my whole 13+ years in business with you but I could be here all day, and this book isn't about me (maybe one day I can share with you, my learnings; the fun, emotion, frustration, disappointment, oh and yes, the Bridget Jones times!), this book is about you, and will provide you with the formula to step forward with your business or brand, to get results, customers, and profits from social media.

Filling the Gap

For now, google me, Zoe Cairns, and you'll find lots of TV and radio interviews, and details of my speaking engagements across the 14 countries I have spoken in, including speaking for NATO and European Parliament and Government. You will also see my passion for travelling.

What you won't see online is the frustration, disappointment, and emotions that I have experienced over the years of running my business. I have put this book together to help the many businesses, entrepreneurs, and social media enthusiasts out there that put a lot of time and resources into their social media activities but feel like they get nowhere. Please don't feel alone. I've been there along with the many other businesses I have helped. This book is a guide, to take you through the key steps that over the years we have defined as a formula for our clients to follow, to become successful online and to navigate the social media maze.

What's Inside: Your Social Media Success Formula

In this book, I would love to share with you my Social Media Success Formula. A formula that has been used over the last few years amongst my clients and mentees and generates the results, leads, and profits they are looking for in their business.

From Basics to Brilliance

Each chapter brings you the elements of each step of the formula, explaining its importance, but more crucially, how you can implement this into your own social media activities. When I say there is something in this book for everyone, I honestly mean it; from a small business looking to discover how to get started, to a social media enthusiast or manager looking to refine their strategy.

Real Stories, Real Results

I will be sharing real stories, real results and real learnings. You will find me completely transparent, and I will share my deepest secrets, pains, and challenges throughout this book. I would like you to learn from my own experiences over the years and for this book to be a quick step forward for your social media activities.

However, this is not a get rich quick book with make money fast schemes. It's a formula to help you refine your social media strategy and to start seeing those results over a long-term plan.

Your Gain: Tailored Tips and Tried-and-True Tactics

Yes, you read the subtitle here right, I will be sharing tips, and tried and true tactics.

For the Small Business Owners: I will be emphasising how a strong social media presence can increase opportunities and your awareness online, allowing you to start getting seen by your target audience but most importantly, start generating leads.

For the Entrepreneurs: I will share insights on how I used social media for personal branding, networking, and leveraging social media to attract investors, customers, and collaborators.

For the Social Media Enthusiasts: I will be sharing my experience of platform algorithms, content strategies, and engagement tactics to turn your passion and knowledge into profits.

How to Navigate: Making the Most of This Book

There are many ways you can use this book.

Dip or Dive: You can read cover to cover, or just go straight to the sections that are most relevant to you, and that you require guidance on. However, I do recommend you work through the book to make note of the 7 key steps of the formula. Even though you might already know a particular step, have a read; you never know, there may be a nugget or gem that you weren't aware of and that you can pick up to implement into your strategy.

Interactive Elements: You can head to the action taking tasks in the book. If you're anything like me, I love taking big action. That's why I have added lots of templates, challenges, and actionable tasks in the book for you to apply what you are learning in real time. Just to add, I would love to hear your progress. Share your progress online and tag me in @zcairns #BeyondTheFeed

Stay Connected: Whilst we are talking about sharing your progress online. I would love you to stay connected. Share your progress, questions, or success stories with me. I love hearing about my community's progress.

Your Next Steps: Ready, Set, Read

Now, you know who I am (well maybe not the Bridget Jones moments yet!), and what to expect from this book, it's now time to get started.

With every page you turn, remember you are a step closer to getting your strategy started or refining your strategy.

Dive in, experiment with my suggested tactics and actions, and have fun!

To Your Successes

Zoe

"Know your 'why', so on those not-so-motivated days, you have something to keep driving and inspiring you."

Chapter Two

Dream Big, Start Smart: Goals and Objectives

Why Bother with Goals?

The first step of the Social Media Success Formula is setting goals. Setting goals is an important part of your social media journey. Without goals you won't know how far you have come or whether your social media activities have actually worked for you or not.

What you don't want to be doing is spending time and resources on something that doesn't work, so therefore it is key to set goals and make sure that you monitor and measure your activities.

As for anything in life, without goals we have nothing to aim for. Setting goals enables you to have a guide, a focus point to aim for.

The goals will keep you on track and will make sure that you don't get distracted by the next shiny new social media platform or get lost amongst the noise online.

Once goals are set you can then create strategies, tactics, and actions to work towards achieving these goals.

What is also great about having goals is that on the days when you're feeling a bit lost or overwhelmed and procrastinating about posting online, remembering your goals can not only give you that much needed push or remind you 'why' you are doing what you are doing, but also what actions you need to take to get you back on track. That motivation boost is exactly what we all need sometimes.

Setting goals that align with your business

The Big Picture

When setting your social media goals, it's so important to make sure they align with what you want to achieve in your business. Otherwise, you will attract the wrong type of business and wonder why things are going wrong.

So... Look at your business goals. What is it you would like to achieve in your business? How can social media help you achieve this?

Many businesses I work with often say to me that, social media doesn't work. When I say to them, "Let's see your social media strategy," specifically their goals, they don't have any. How do they know it's not working for them when they haven't set goals to measure their activity?

The other thing is that some of them don't have a business plan for their business. This can then become difficult. If they don't know what they want to achieve in their business, how can they use social media to help? They need to know their ambitions for their business, have a business plan and then set their goals for their social media activities.

This alignment between planning, goals, and strategy, means that you can then start getting your social media activities working for you, which will ultimately help your business grow and succeed in the way you would like it to.

When thinking about what you would like to achieve in your business, think specifically about revenue, attracting clients, expansion, and work-life balance and so on. Use these goals to create or revise your business plan and then start to think about how social media can help you to meet these goals and objectives.

The Three Goals of Social Media Success

When setting social media goals, I always get my clients to look at three key areas to start with. These three areas will enable you to build a 'know, like and trust' strategy.

I'm going to break down the three areas and share with you how you can set your goals within each area.

Awareness

Awareness is all about getting your brand online and getting in front of your target audience.

Until you build awareness, your target audience will not be familiar with who you are, or what you do. The importance of awareness is being consistent. Start sharing your thought leadership with regular posting and by sharing good quality content that your target audience will find useful.

Getting your message out there and being seen by your audience will start to get people seeing you on a regular basis and recognising your name or brand. This will start to establish a 'know' factor.

Setting a goal to build your online awareness is a good starting point, because until people know who you are, you won't get your message out to the audience you are looking to target.

Establish your **impressions** (the total number of times people see you online) and **reach** (the unique number of times people see you online) to start getting seen and begin building an online community.

Remember first impression matters. Make sure that you have thought about your key messages and how you plan on educating, entertaining and engaging with your audience.

Building awareness is all about creating strategies that keep you at the forefront of the minds and feeds of your target audience.

Build Community

The great thing about social media is that it gives us the opportunity to get our brand and message in front of thousands, or even millions of people who could potentially be our ideal customers. However, it's become more difficult to get people to 'like' or 'follow' our page as people prefer to scroll past and reduce the 'noise' in their feeds.

This is why it's so important to make sure that the content you are sharing is of good value, engaging, or entertaining. This will encourage your potential customers to click on that 'like' or 'follow' to continue to see your posts in the future.

Setting a goal that is based on building your community is key. But I don't want you to get carried away with vanity metrics of setting goals for thousands and thousands of followers. "Why," you ask? Well, you could have thousands of followers but none of them may actually engage or buy. Or you could have a smaller engaged audience that convert. I know what I would prefer... the latter!

When setting a community building goal make sure that it is realistic. It's important not to get disheartened by unrealistic short-term goals, but to gradually grow a community within your target audience that you can manage, to engage, nurture, and have conversations with. I call it the art of turning 'likes' into 'conversations'.

To build a community, or a raving fan base, you need to create content that stands out. Content that doesn't just get the thumbs tapping, but sparks conversations that will result in conversions.

Remember, it's all about a targeted, *engaged* audience, it's not about numbers. This is the stage during which your audience starts to like you, follow you, and will be ready for when you share your key messages.

Conversations and Conversions

The third goal I always get the businesses I'm working with to set is **traffic and conversions**. Once your audience get to know you via you building awareness, they will then follow you and start to like your content. After that, as you build their trust, you will create opportunities to drive them to your website, offer, or a DM for a conversation - all leading to that ultimate conversion.

However, it's so, so important to make sure that you have mapped out your customer journey first. I've had consultations with a few clients who have such amazing engagement and conversations with their audience but struggle with the conversions because they have failed to complete this vital step in their strategic planning.

You need to monitor and analyse what works for you. Do you give too much away that your customer then feels they don't need to buy from you? Or do you fail to hook them in with your content, meaning that they don't have that real *need* to purchase? Do they visit your website and then drop off as you don't take them to the place they need to go? Perhaps your content isn't aligning with the website or landing page you have taken them to?

In the first three months of setting your goals, monitoring your website traffic and conversations would be a focus I would concentrate on. Then, from month three to six, start thinking about the conversions once your audience have built that 'know, like, and trust'.

Building trust with your audience is so important to the foundation of any conversion. Make sure that you are having meaningful conversations and monitoring the engagement on your social media activities; failing to do this could mean that you are not missing out on missed opportunities and conversions.

Three Goal Examples to Get You Started

You're probably thinking, "Ok this is great, but I wouldn't have a clue where to start with my goals or what to set that is realistic."

I always tell my clients when I am working with them to keep their goals **SMART**. Have you ever heard of SMART goals?

SMART stands for **S**pecific, **M**easurable, **A**ttainable, **R**ealistic and **T**imely. When you set your goals go through the SMART acronym and make sure you are keeping to each one.

I thought I would share three goals that are SMART that you all could try setting to get you started:

Increase your online brand awareness by 10% each month – this is going to make sure you get seen by your audience and start to make your name known. You can measure this by monitoring the **impressions** and **reach** of your posts.

Build your community within your target audience by 10% each month – this is going to help you build a community of people that will not only increase engagement and conversations, but most importantly create a raving fan base that is starting to like your content and build trust for when you share those offers and promotions.

You can measure this goal by monitoring the increase in your page likes, follows, engagement rate, and conversations in your inbox.

To make sure that your community is made up of your desired target audience, you can check the metrics on the demographics, locations, and interests of your audience in the analytics of each social media platform. It is important to monitor this to make sure that your activities are attracting your target audience – i.e., the right audience for your product or service.

Increase your website traffic by 10% or **increase your engagement** rate by 10%. You could choose one or both goals as these will start establishing trust with your audience and lead to conversations that you can begin to turn into conversions.

 Website traffic and engagement can be measured by monitoring the following analytics:

- Social traffic in your google analytics will show you the amount of website traffic you receive from your social media activities. If you have access to your website, you can also use Google URL shorten which will enable you to be more specific in tracking the traffic from specific posts, but ultimately to track what posts are getting the conversions for you. This will help you to track more in-depth information and understand exactly which posts are generating traffic to your website or sales.

- Another metric to measure and monitor these two goals is your engagement rate. Your engagement rate is key to the success of building your community but also establishing trust. I find this to be a better metric to use than the number of followers, as it actually tells you how engaged your audience are. Aim for a 10% increase in comments and shares over the next month.

And finally monitor your conversions. Remember social media takes time and should be a long-term strategy. It's not an overnight win. Therefore, initial conversion goals should be monitored and measured via conversations in your inbox or through building your email list of warm leads as an example.

Now It's Your Turn

Now I've explained goal setting and given you some SMART examples, it's your turn. I would love you to take action and complete the following task:

Note down the three goals that you are going to set and would love to achieve over the next three months. You can use my examples, tweak them, or use them in their exact form.

Remember, dream big but start SMART.

Once you've got them noted down, you're all set to move onto the next chapter.

Share your goals online with the hashtag #BeyondTheFeed and tag @zcairns in!

"Don't let anyone hold you back from your dreams.
Set your goals, keep focused and be amazing!"

Chapter Three

Understanding Your Target Audience

Why Bother with a Target Audience?

When using social media or doing any sort of marketing, it's really important to make sure that you understand who your target audience are. Who are the people that need your product or service? What pain or challenge do they have that is creating the need to buy your product or service and solve the problem?

If you don't know who your target audience are, how do you know whether your product or service would be in demand? And this is why it is so important to find out about your audience's pains and challenges first before creating the product or service; this will ensure that there is a demand for it when you finally launch.

Lots of people steam ahead and get on every social media platform out there. They presume that getting on every platform is best. However, it is important to make sure that once you define who your target audience are, you can then choose the right platforms; the places where your target audience are spending time together. Otherwise, you could waste a lot of time and resources posting in places that your target audience are not frequenting.

Identifying your audience is key to choosing the right social media platforms to use, post and engage on.

This also saves you time in the future. When a new social media platform emerges, understanding your target audience means you can make the right decision as to whether your audience are engaging and present on that platform, and whether it is right for your strategy.

Spotlight Focus

So, how do you start defining who your target audience are? I always say to my clients and mentees when thinking about defining their target audience, think about the clients you already have and create a buyer persona of who they are.

What are their interests, why do they buy your products or services? What are their pains and challenges? We will talk about this in more detail later in the chapter. But I want you to start thinking about those current clients that you currently have. Who is your ideal client, and just as importantly, who is not your ideal client? Note these details down, as these will really help you define who your target audience are.

When you know who you are talking to, you waste less time and money on messages that do not resonate.

The Magic of Knowing Your Crowd

The Big Why

I've had so many people say to me, "I don't need to define who my audience are, I know who they are." My response: "If you know exactly who they are, why aren't your social media activities getting the results you are looking for?"

When we begin to break down their target audience and start to discuss their audience's pains and challenges, they soon realise then that either the messaging and content they have been creating and posting is not what their audience want to see, or if it's resonating with them. In this case, their audience isn't taking action.

Audience Blueprint: To help and assist with this part of your strategy I have created a target audience sheet. You can download this from the website http://www.beyondthefeed.com

Completing Your Target Audience Sheet

Your very own Target Audience Sheet will assist you with many activities in both your business and marketing. It is useful when creating new campaigns or thinking about new products.

It is also useful when deciding to use social media advertising (paid social) when creating an audience for your advert; this assists and helps you more strategically as you already have the details from your audience sheet rather than guessing!

I recommend you update the target audience sheet regularly, ideally every quarter, to ensure that you are updating any new trends, interests, or pains and challenges for your audience.

Add an action in your diary every 12 weeks (about 3 months) along with your 90-day planning schedule (we will talk about this later in the book) to make sure that you regularly visit your target audience sheet.

Audience Avatar

Your target audience sheet helps you to create a detailed profile of your ideal customer or follower. Like I said earlier, if you go blank and struggle to think about the details, think of an existing customer and their particular interests and demographics.

Beyond Demographics

The sheet gets you to think about not only the age or location of your ideal customer, but also to think about their hobbies, interests, magazines they read, radio shows they listen to, associations and professional bodies they may be part of, where they network or who they may already follow.

Why is this all important? It is important as it gives you the opportunity to find out more about your audience. It provides you with an insight into what they might be interested to see on their feed. Not only what they would like to engage in, but also where you might find them online.

For example, You may be looking to get in front of HR consultants who would be members of a specific HR association. By looking for this association on social media, you will then be able to find your target audience and what they are engaging with.

Or it could be that you are a pet grooming business, looking for pet owners in your local area. What other pet businesses, activities, or groups would they be following or engaging with?

Walking in Their Shoes

Pains and Gains

Understanding the pains and challenges of your audience can shape your messaging for your social media content.

When speaking to your audience and making them feel like you know and understand how they feel, or the challenges they are experiencing, they will relate to your content and also start to establish that 'know like and trust' factor with you or your brand.

When your content specifically directs them to a call to action, where you are providing a solution to their pain and challenge, this is when you will see results from your social media activities. You must have a strategy to find out what those pains and challenges are.

There are a few ways you can do this. Firstly, get yourself a little notebook, or open a shared google doc with your team. Title it: 'Target audience pains and challenges'.

Now, every time a potential or existing customer asks you a question or has a challenge, write this onto your google doc, as these are your audience's pains and challenges. All of these can create useful content! I will explain later how you can use them to create content that your audience will love.

Alternatively, if you are more visual, or have a whiteboard in your office, you can use post-it notes and have a brainstorming hour where you note down all the questions, pains, and challenges and keep adding them to the whiteboard. You can then start mapping them out and create a content plan with them.

Tools and Tricks to Know Them Better

Digital Detective Work

There are some tools out there that you can use to identify your target audience's pains and challenges. I always recommend, however, doing the whiteboard and post-it note exercise first.

Sometimes though, it is easy to become stuck, and yourself be challenged with this exercise. Just getting ideas from a few useful tools can give you that creative spark and initial push to get you started on noting down those pains and challenges.

I have a few online tools I would love to share with you:

Answerthepublic.com When I first was introduced to this tool, I thought wow! How amazing is this? A tool that gives you some great questions and ideas. The tool works alongside Google. By working with Google, it brings together all the questions your target audience is asking about a particular topic or subject.

You type in your topic or subject, and it brings up a mind map of all the questions. At the beginning of each question in the inner circle it shows little orange circles. The darker the orange the more people that are asking this question.

These questions can be formed as social media posts, videos, blogs, reels, lead magnets, email newsletter topics, and much more.

As these are the key questions your audience is asking, if you provide content and the solution to these questions, this will attract your audience to your content and resonate with them so that they will engage or take the call to action on your post.

You will really build a 'know, like and trust' with your audience.

Answerthepublic.com has a free element to it. If you register a free account, you get around 2-3 free searches a day. This is more than enough for you to do some initial research.

Google Search

Google is another useful tool which will also provide you with some of the key questions that people are asking Google about a particular topic or subject.

Go to Google.com and type in the search bar a question about your product or service.

It will then share a list of websites that you can visit to find out more, however, you will find a list of questions amongst the list of websites.

These are questions that others are also asking about this topic or subject. The great thing about this also, is that when you click on one question, it then expands and shows more questions too. You can gather so many pains and challenges from this to add to your whiteboard or document for content and messaging research.

Quora.com Quora is a forum where people gather to ask various questions about topics and interests. You only get a couple of searches before it asks you to create a free account, this will then enable you to use it further.

It is great for giving you a different perspective on how people respond to the questions asked and about their challenges as well.

YouTube.com YouTube shares videos that have been created to answer specific questions and challenges your audience may have. Again, this is useful to find out the top content topics people are creating; you could also add to this from a different perspective or collect ideas on what types of videos you can create for your audience that would answer their specific questions.

Google Jamboard: Jamboard is a tool that is an online whiteboard allowing you to add digital post-it notes. If you are a paperless company, passionate about sustainability, then Jamboard is the perfect tool to help you keep your ideas online. Jamboard is completely free to use. You can access it via your Google account. You can also share it with team members and get them to add their ideas and suggestions too, just like a Google document.

Lastly, **Pinterest.com**: Pinterest shares creative ideas along with what others have created to answer their audiences' pains and challenges. From infographics to checklists and useful eBooks, Pinterest can give you ideas on different content types that you can create to engage with your target audience.

What tool will you use? When sharing these with my clients and mentees, I encourage them to give them all a try to experience different ideas and opportunities.

Feedback Gold

If you already have an established audience, customer database and a mailing list, this is a fantastic opportunity to get to know your audience better by reaching out with surveys, feedback forms and having direct conversations.

One way this has worked well with some of my current mentees is by doing a survey but having a reward or competition to entice people to take part. For example: you may have seen this before where, if you complete a survey, you will then be entered into a competition.

Make sure the competition is something they your audience would find beneficial and will want to complete the survey for.

The survey can ask them key questions about their pains, challenges, interests, and hobbies.

Try not to make the survey too long, otherwise this will deter your audience away as people don't have massive amounts of time. Keep it short, concise, and think about the key things you want to get out of it.

I would recommend 2-3 questions in the survey. These could be:

1. What is your biggest challenge with 'topic'?

2. What would you love to learn about 'topic'?

3. What would your ultimate outcome be with 'topic'?

These are some question ideas that will help you get to understand your audience far better. I even use these questions when engaging with my audience before they join a Facebook group or when creating an online challenge or webinar they would like to attend. It enables me to form the content and structure of that session.

Even before creating an online course, launching a new service, or a new product, I would create a survey and send it to my audience first before spending too much time and resources on something that they might not require. This is a cost-effective way to find out about your audience who are already engaging and following you.

Stay Updated

As mentioned earlier in the chapter; people change - your target audience preferences, interests, and challenges change based on trends, climate, environment, business growth, and much more. This is why it is so important to regularly update your target audience sheet. We recommend revisiting every 12 weeks (about 3 months) to account for these changes.

Your Action Plan!

Now that I've shared all this knowledge and useful tools, it's now time for you to start completing your target audience sheet but also identifying their pains and challenges.

I would love you to download the target audience sheet and start thinking about your audience's demographics and interests. Think about your ideal follower or customer. You can do this by thinking about your current customers and followers, and what they may have shared with you in conversation about their interests, who they follow, etc.

I would then like you to start forming a mind map of their pains and challenges. Firstly, gather some post-it notes and think about the frequent questions that your potential or existing customers ask you, add these to a whiteboard, or a tool like Google Jamboard.

Once you've down this you're now ready to start tailoring your messages and content to resonate with your audience, they will find this content useful, engaging, and trust that you know how they feel and understand what they need!

The better you know your audience, the better chances you have of turning those casual feed scrollers into your ravings fans and converting them into customers.

Take a screenshot of your research and target audience sheet and share online with the hashtag #BeyondTheFeed and tag @zcairns in!

"To create engaging content that resonates and prompts your ideal customer to take action, get to know your audience well! Understand their pains and challenges and how you can help them with a solution!"

Chapter Four

Creating Irresistible Lead Magnets

Now, that you know your target audience and what their pains and challenges are, it's time to start getting in front of them and grabbing their attention. Being equipped with their challenges, you are ready to create your very own lead magnet which will provide them with a solution and enable you to nurture them and convert them into a customer.

What's a Lead Magnet Anyway?

A 'lead magnet' is simply a special offer or incentive that businesses give to potential customers in exchange for their contact information, usually their email address. Think of it as the freebie you get when you sign up for something.

For example, if a website offers a free downloadable guide or eBook in return for you subscribing to their email newsletter, that guide or eBook is the 'lead magnet'. The business can then use your contact information to follow up with you, often with more information, offers, or promotions, related to their products or services.

I bet if you think about the last thing you signed up to, you got something in exchange for giving your name and email address. Whether it was 5% off or an eBook or a guide about a new hobby.

Over the years I have loved lead magnets, as it has given me a real insight into the mentor, coach, service, or sample of the product before the investment.

The Exchange

You're probably thinking why collect a name and email address? Why not just give the guide or eBook away? Well, have you ever heard of the saying, 'The money is in your list?' If you haven't then it's time to consider a lead magnet.

We spend so much time and resources getting in front of our audiences across social media. Our audience may like, comment, and engage, but, because of the algorithms, our audience might not see all our posts, making it more difficult to show up regularly in front of them. However, if you have a list, you can email your list on a consistent basis and land in their inbox with the latest news, offer, or content, thereby nurturing your potential customers.

And before I go on... I can hear you say, "What if it lands in their junk folder!" I'll share a tip about this later in the chapter.

You can build your list with the power of social media by creating a lead magnet. You create something that provides a solution to your audience's pain or challenge, your audience is attracted to the lead magnet because you are offering a solution to their burning pain or challenge, they then download your freebie, in exchange for their name and email address; you have now added a potential lead to your list, someone who is an ideal customer for you because they have 'bought in' to your offer. Now you can follow up and nurture them with your regular emails.

This exchange of information in return for your solution-based lead magnet is a valuable exchange. By building your list you have a list of potential customers who are looking for the help and guidance that your service or product can provide.

And this is why they say, 'the money is in the list', as you can start to work out an average conversion when emailing your list. A known statistic is that sending an email, leads to an average conversion rate of 3-5% (Source: Mailchimp).

Audience First: Tailoring Your Magnet

Know Their Pains: For your lead magnet to be successful you need to make sure that your lead magnet is solving a solution for your target audience. In the previous chapter, we covered how to understand the pains and challenges of your target audience.

This understanding will enable you to create a lead magnet that will provide your audience with valuable content and information that they can put into action and address. This will build a 'know, like and trust' relationship with the potential customer, accelerating their buying potential.

There are many tools that will help you to understand what the pains and challenges might be, and if you haven't read chapter 2, I would urge you to go back and read it as it's so important that those actions are covered before planning and creating your lead magnet.

A Custom Fit

Creating a lead magnet that answers specific pains and challenges of your target audience can increase its appeal and lead to higher engagement. Here are some tips to help you plan your lead magnet effectively:

1. **Know your audience:** Before creating a lead magnet you need to make sure you have an understanding of who your target

audience is. Complete your target audience analysis, which will include all of their demographics, interests, challenges, and goals.

2. **Solve a problem:** Your lead magnet should offer a solution to a problem or challenge that your audience has. For example, recently I helped a client whose audience was struggling with time management, so they created an eBook with productivity hacks and recommendations for time tracking tools.

3. **Make it relevant:** Make sure that the lead magnet you create and offer, is relevant to the products or services that you provide, otherwise you will build a list of people who are not your ideal customer.

4. **Keep it specific:** Try not to go off on a tangent. Keep your lead magnet simple and specific. You don't want to overwhelm your audience with too much information or overwhelm them so much that they don't put your advice into action. This could have a negative effect and deter them from the buying experience with you moving forward.

5. **Keep it engaging:** There are many different types of lead magnets so make sure that you choose a type that will best present your content and appeal the most to your audience. It is crucial that you keep them engaged.

6. **Catchy title:** Make sure that your title is speaking directly to your target audience's pain or challenge; you need them to immediately to see that you understand them and compel them to download.

7. **Add social proof:** Make sure you add testimonials or case studies that not only relate to the lead magnet, but also to the services

and products you provide. If it's an eBook for example, you can include reviews from readers who found it useful.

The Magnet Menu: Types of Lead Magnets

The Variety

There are so many different types of lead magnets, the list is endless. However, it's important to choose a type of lead magnet that your particular audience will engage with and find interesting.

I am going to give you the different types but also provide a pro and con for each type as well. Remember it all depends on your audience and content as to which lead magnet would be more appropriate for you to use – one size does not fit all!

1. **eBooks**

    Pros: A great way to go into more depth with your topic and can position you as an expert in your field. These can be shared consistently, but also if they have evergreen content (content that doesn't go out of date), they will last longer and not require constant updating.
    Cons: Can be time consuming to create. Your audience may not have the time to read something lengthy.

2. **Cheat Sheets or Checklists**

    Pros: Quick to create and offers actionable value for your audience. They are much easier and faster to create than an eBook.

Cons: A cheat sheet or checklist doesn't give you the opportunity to go into depth into your topic areas. Therefore, your audience might not see them as much value as eBooks.

3. **Templates**

Pros: Creating templates that your target audience can use means you are saving your audience time, and they can use them over and over again!
Cons: If your templates are for a specific industry, these templates may need updating over time.

4. **Webinars**

Pros: Webinars enable your target audience to have personal interaction with you and the opportunity to ask their questions positioning you as an expert in your field. Webinars can also be repurposed into other forms of content.
Cons: Doing Webinars is both time consuming and time sensitive as it requires you to be there each time unless you use tools like EasyWebinar which enables you to have a recorded webinar on autopilot and for your audience to choose a convenient time and date to view. A great feature is that your audience can still ask questions which will come to you directly, and you can respond. However, if you are not tech savvy you may be required to learn new skills.

5. **Free Trials and Offers**

Pros: It allows your potential clients to try out your product or service, a great way to introduce them to your brand. It gives you the opportunity to then upsell and accelerate the buying potential with your customer.

Cons: This may not be cost effective as some of your products may not be suitable for trials. Also, you'll need to make sure you have a strategy for the follow up process in order to be able to upsell or to get those people trialling your product/service to buy further from you moving forward.

6. Quizzes or Surveys

Pros: Quizzes are a great lead magnet that are both engaging and interactive. They can also provide some useful information about your audience that you can use for future developments and research.

Cons: When creating quizzes or surveys you need a tool or platform that will help you host the quiz or survey. Again, this may require certain tech skills and also might not be seen as high value to your audience unless you provide a follow up with this particular lead magnet, such as a detailed email about their result. A great tool that I can recommend here is Daniel Priestley's Scorecard.

7. Online Courses, Challenges or Facebook Groups

Pros: By providing an online course, you are able to give a sneak peek or taster of your complete courses or packages and build a relationship with your potential customers. You can then tempt your audience to upgrade and purchase the full course. By 'dripping' content to your audience, you can keep them engaged over a certain time period and establish trust.

Cons: The downside to this strategy, is that it requires consistent content creations and updates. You also need to make sure that you are following up in case your audience start to lose interest and drop off. A couple of examples of this are online challenges and Facebook groups.

8. Video Tutorials or Series

Pros: Videos are visually engaging for your audience and can help you explain a topic that needs more explanation or demonstration; using videos means that your content can be easily shared. They can also enable your audience to establish trust with you more quickly.

Cons: Creating videos is time consuming and if you hire someone to record them for you then it can also cost you as well. However, you can produce these yourself with various available tools. You will also need to consider where your videos will be hosted or use a platform that is easily accessible.

9. Discounts or Special Offers

Pros: Providing discounts and special offers gives your potential customers an incentive to purchase and are easy to implement, especially if you have an online shop via ecommerce websites where you can provide a discount code.

Cons: When giving too many discounts and special offers this can not only reduce your profit margins, but also mean that your audience may become accustomed to waiting until you have a discount or special offer rather than buying at full price.

10. Reports or Whitepapers

Pros: Creating reports and whitepapers are great for business to business (B2B) audiences. They can showcase research and expertise and will often have a high perceived value by your target audience.

Cons: They can be time consuming to produce as they are lengthy and cover a lot of detail, including statistics. Due to the need to add insights and statistics, they may need regularly updating.

Choosing the right lead magnet for your target audience and aligning it with your business goals is so important to make sure you achieve the required engagement and conversion for your business.

A few examples:

- For B2B businesses who are looking to target the decision makers in a business or organisation, creating lead magnets such as detailed whitepapers or research reports will showcase their authority and offer good value. Alternatively, an eCommerce business might choose special offers or discounts to drive immediate sales.

- If you are a business that is looking to educate or build your audience awareness around a particular topic, you might choose webinars or online courses for engagement but also to establish trust and to educate your audience before making the buying decision.

- Startups introducing a new software tool might look at offering free trials or demos, targeting potential long-term users of the software; here you also have the opportunity of upselling.

By understanding the specific needs of your target audience along with your business goals, you can choose the right lead magnet that will not only grab your audience's attention but also get them taking the actions that are aligned with your set goals.

Creative Tools: Making Your Magnet Shine

DIY Friendly

There are so many tools out there that you can use to create your lead magnet. I am going to share a few of them with you to get your started. You don't need to be a designer or a tech expert to use these as many of them have step by step wizards; there are so many video tutorials on YouTube to guide you through as well.

Canva - A designing tool which has many available templates to help you create your lead magnets such as eBooks, checklists, cheat sheets, planners and much more.

Attract.io - A hosting tool where you can create and host your lead magnet; ideal for quick creation and getting your lead magnet out there.

EasyWebinar - A webinar platform that enables you to host and run live and automated webinars.

Zoom - A great tool to get you started with live webinars. You can also use zoom to record video tutorials and demonstrations.

Vimeo or YouTube - Both of these tools I would recommend for hosting your video content that you wish to share with your audience.

Scorecard - If you're looking to do a quiz then this is a tool you can use to share it with your audience and capture their data.

Once you have created your lead magnet you then need to consider how you will host it and also what email marketing software you will use to create your email form to start collecting the audience data. This email marketing software will enable you to set up an automation that will automatically send your lead magnet to your audience when they sign up for your lead magnet.

To learn more about this visit http://www.beyondthefeed.com

Spreading the Word: Promoting Your Lead Magnet

Visibility is Key

When your lead magnet is ready to go and you're ready to start building a list of warm leads, it's time to use social media to help you promote it.

There are so many ways you can promote your lead magnet; however, the key is consistency. You need to consistently share your lead magnet multiple times in order for your promotion to be a successful process.

I've had a few mentees who have said, "It's not working." I then say, "How many times have you shared it?" and they say, "Once." This is not enough! You need to ensure that your lead magnet promotion is part of your social media content plan. It's a campaign that should be ongoing unless your lead magnet is time sensitive and has a certain shelf-life. An example of this is that I have an ongoing advert that is continuously running to promote my lead magnet and grow my email list. Before this, I was spending around £200-£250 on regular magazine and paper adverts but now would prefer to invest this amount on social advertising. I spend on average £100 per month now and generate around 65-100 people to my list each month. This is just on one lead magnet.

My lead magnet is getting in front of my ideal audience and is an important part of my awareness and growth strategy,

I will say though, we've had some amazing successes in the ZC Social Media Growth Academy; one of which was for a member who put out her first post for her lead magnet on Instagram, and to her amazement she gained 93 subscribers to her email list! This was a great success for her as she was then able to nurture these subscribers and upsell to her membership.

Multi-Channel Approach

As mentioned earlier, consistency is key, but also having a multi-channel approach sharing your lead magnet is equally important.

Don't just share your lead magnet on one of the platforms available, share them where your target audience are active, but also utilise the different features on the platform. For example, share a post on your Instagram grid, but also create a story template to promote your lead magnet, and go LIVE to share with your audience! There are so many opportunities to get it out there.

There are many ways you can promote your lead magnet; it doesn't just have to be a promotional post. Here are just some of the ways you can promote your lead magnet:

Stories: Use Facebook and Instagram stories to promote your lead magnet. From questions to stories asking if people would like your download, a template story with a link sticker, or a selfie video with a link.

LIVE: Go LIVE and share some good content with your audience and ask them to type 'download' in the comments for you to then send them your download. You can add the link to the caption or even use a chatbot like 'Manychat' that will automatically send them the download!

Add to your bio: You can have up to five links in your Instagram bio, add your download link there. Also, make sure you have added your lead magnet link to your social media profiles bios.

Create a carousel: Share an educational carousel post, on the end slide, share a call to action to download your lead magnet to learn more.

These are just a couple of the many opportunities you have to promote your lead magnet. I could go on... but these will get you started.

If you're interested, I have created a free download on http://www.beyondthefeed.com which is a 30-day calendar with an action each day to help you share your lead magnet.

Ok... I can hear you... You want more ideas on where to share your lead magnet? Oh go on then...! I have created a 30-day calendar with an action each day on where you can share your lead magnet.

If you like a challenge, work towards your first 100 subscribers by downloading the calendar from http://www.beyondthefeed.com

Your Action Plan: Time to Brainstorm!

It's now your turn to take action on what you have learned. I would love you to brainstorm what your lead magnet could be. I would like you to think back to Chapter 2 and look at your audience's pains and challenges. Which one could you provide a solution for?

Jot down your ideas, sketch out some concepts and get your creative juices flowing. Remember, the best lead magnet is one that helps and resonates with its audience!

When you start marketing your lead magnet, make sure you tag me in! @zcairns #beyondthefeed

"Share your
best content
freely and fully.
In giving, we create
connections, trust, and
unexpected paths to
success."

Chapter Five

Creating Content: Making Posts That Resonate and Engage

One of the key elements of being successful on social media is making sure you have a consistent marketing message that resonates with and engages your audience. Your content is what is going to get the attention of your audience and encourage them to take action. Poor content = poor social media results.

I have a structure that I share with my mentees that they follow to create their social media content plans. The success of this structure has led me to create a social media planner that is shared with thousands of people all over the world.

I would love to share this structure with you here. Let's get into it.

Zooming In: Defining Your Business Focus

Spotlight on Services/Products: First of all, I would like you to think about the specific services or products that you would like to champion on social media. I would start with two or three to get started.

One of the key things you can push is your lead magnet, as ultimately you can nurture your audience and upsell to the key service or product you wish to push.

Some of you will have different products or services that you will push at different times of the year, or seasonally. Therefore, it's always recommended to update your content plan every 90 days (12 weeks). It is for this reason that you may have seen me speak about 90-Day

Content Planning, or if you own one of my planners you will see it has four sections of 90-Days for this very purpose.

Why It Matters: People always say, "Why can't I promote every service or product I have?" The answer I give them is that if you try to push too many, your message can become too diluted, and your audience won't know what action to take. But also, it's important to think about the product/service ladder journey of your ideal customer.

Your Product/Service Ladder is the mapping out of the journey throughout which your ideal customer would purchase one product or service, and then would transition or upgrade to another.

Whereabouts on the ladder would you like to attract your ideal audience on social media? How can you then upsell to your audience to transition them to the next level?

What many businesses and entrepreneurs do is try to sell their high-ticket product or service straight out on social media. This can be challenging if the audience haven't established a 'know, like and trust' relationship with you, and most certainly if they are at the beginning of the buyer journey with you. This is why you will see that some businesses and entrepreneurs offer a FREE Webinar or FREE download to establish that know, like and trust and to then upsell to their interested and engaged audience.

Brainstorming: Topics Galore

With the chosen services or products you would like to focus on, I would like you to take each service and create a mind map.

For each service or product, brainstorm all the relevant topics they cover. For example: if you are an accountant and you have chosen Annual Tax Return Submission for your key service, you could come up with the following topics associated with this: deadlines, things you can claim against, accountancy jargon, different types of income, deductions, investments, and much more.

The Gold in Details

By brainstorming your service and product topics you are uncovering so many content ideas for your plan. When I go through this process with my mentees, normally at the beginning of the content planning session, one of their pains and challenges is, they never know what to post. With this process you will discover endless content opportunities.

If you are working with a team, I always suggest doing this exercise via Google Jamboard as you can then share the mind map with your other team members and also get them to contribute their ideas too. Allow this to be an ongoing working document that you can keep adding to it.

Addressing Pains and Challenges

Once you have your topics, you can then start exploring each topic and finding your target audience's pains and challenges based on each one. In Chapter 2, we covered this in quite a bit of detail, and I also shared various tools that you can use to find the pains and challenges of your audience.

For this section, I would take one topic at a time, and write down all of the pains and challenges they would have under each topic. This ends up looking like a topic at the top of a box with multiple questions underneath it. Each of these questions can become a piece of content.

When creating the questions, make sure you think about not only addressing their pains and challenges, but also providing them with key tips, and snippets of useful information that will offer a solution. This will really make your brand stand out and accelerate that know like and trust relationship with your audience.

Mixing Up Your Post Types

When creating content, it's important to make sure that you use different types of content across your social media platforms in order to monitor what type of posts resonate with your audience and what gets them engaged the most.

There are so many different ways you can present your content. I am going to share a few of the options available.

Text posts: Simple written updates or status messages without any multimedia elements such as pictures or videos.

Image posts: Single images or photos with or without captions. These are the most basic visual posts.

Video posts: Videos of varying lengths, from short clips to longer-form content, often with captions or descriptions.

Link shares: Posts that share web links to articles, blog posts, videos, or other connections content.

Carousel posts: These posts allow you to include multiple images or videos within a single post, which users can swipe through.

Document posts: Typically, longer form written content shared on social media platforms. They can include articles, reports, case studies, or any text-based document.

Poll posts: Interactive posts that allow you to ask questions and gather feedback from your audience.

Memes and gifs: Humorous or relatable images, animations, or short videos that often go viral.

LIVE video: Real-time video streaming where you can interact with your audience in real time. Available on platforms like Facebook Live, Instagram Live, and YouTube Live.

Stories: Short-lived posts that appear at the top of a user's feed and disappear after 24 hours. Common on platforms like Instagram, Facebook, and Snapchat.

Reels: Video reels are a series of short video clips or scenes, often set to music, and designed to tell a story or capture attention quickly.

User generated content: Posts that feature content created by your audience, such as customer reviews, testimonials, or photos of your product in use.

There are many more, these are just a selection of some of the key post types you can integrate into your content plan.

I always suggest you have an initial content plan that integrates various post types to see what resonates with your audience the most and gets them engaged. At the end of each month, you can then select the post types that worked best with your audience and provide more of the same.

Also, by using a variety of different types of posts, you will keep your audience engaged and avoid them becoming bored as you're not always using the same types of content. If they become bored with the 'sameness' of your posts, you will lose their interaction and this will ultimately affect the algorithms and the chances of them seeing you in their feed.

Keep your content fresh and engaging. Make sure that you are keeping up to date with the latest trends and updates in social media and that you are aware of any algorithm changes that could affect the type of content that you are sharing, which ultimately can affect your results.

Every month I run a Social Media Trends and Updates webinar with my Growth Academy members. This is to inform them of any trending post types and updates with the algorithm, to make sure they are keeping ahead.

Timing is Everything: When and How Often to Post

The Perfect Time

One of the questions I am asked often is, "What is the best time to post on social media?" My response is, "It depends on who your audience are."

Now, when you are starting out on social media and are new to posting for your business, I recommend you vary the timing of your posts over the first month to then discover the best times. The reason being that, if you post at the same time every day, your analytics will have only trialled your content at that time and then give that time as the best time. Therefore, it's advisable to vary the time of posting, to then discover what content did best and what time it was posted.

There are some good tools out there. Most social media management tools will have a feature that gives you the best time to post, based on when your audience is online. We use a tool called Metricool; when selecting in the calendar the day and time you wish to schedule your post, it will highlight parts of the calendar in different shades of blue. The darker the blue, the better the time to post and when your audience are mostly online.

I will add though, even if you do have one of these features in your management tool, for the first month, vary the timing of your posts, see what works best with your audience by doing this organically and analysing your metrics at the end of the month.

The biggest tip I can give you, especially when using Instagram, is to engage with your audience a good 15-20 minutes before you post. This will get your audience looking at your comments on their posts and then coming across to your account to see who you are, and what you are up to, etc. The algorithm will then acknowledge that they are interested in seeing more of your content and show your newly posted post in their feed!

Consistency is Key

You've probably heard this many times, not just from me but from others in the digital marketing space, that consistency is key. It's important to remain present but without overwhelming your followers with too many posts.

However, due to the algorithms, your audience won't see all of your posts, all of the time. It depends on how often they engage with you, which ultimately depends on how engaging your content is.

There are many 'Gurus' out there that will say you need to be posting more than five times a day across every single social media platform. As a small business owner, that can sound overwhelming and the thought of creating that much content seems daunting.

Being consistent doesn't mean you need to be posting five times a day with lots of new content. Consistency is showing up and sharing good quality content. It's about the quality not the quantity. I always say to my mentees, start with posting three times a week, but focus on the quality of your posts.

If you are then finding this manageable, step it up and get to posting daily. Also, remember to use a variety of posts to make sure you are making the best use of all the features of that particular platform to not only reach your audience effectively, but also to get in front of them with the type of content they are mostly engaging with.

To remain consistent, you can use a social media management tool to plan, schedule and keep track of your metrics. Pre planning your content enables you to take advantage of any upcoming opportunities, campaigns, and awareness days, that you might have otherwise missed if not planned.

Post Categories: Generic, Reactive, and Campaign

When pre-planning social media content, I always break down the different categories of posts for my mentees, in order for them to get an idea about how they can be more effective with their social media content plans.

The Basics

By breaking down your content to the following three categories, this will help you plan, create, and post your content more effectively. I am going to share the categories here.

Generic: Generic content is content that won't change and can be created in advance and scheduled into your social media management tool. This normally consists of article posts, service, and product posts, that are normally evergreen. An example of content that wouldn't work for this is a weather post. You wouldn't schedule a post about the weather in a week's time in case it changes and then that post is incorrect. Generic posts could also be planned awareness day posts too.

Reactive: Reactive content is content that is posted as it occurs and can't be planned because you don't have the content until that day; conversely, you couldn't post it after that day as it would then be out of date. For this content you can add an alert in your planner to make sure you capture something on that day and post LIVE. We normally recommend having a WhatsApp group with your team to share this content and also send reminders for them to capture content.

Campaigns: Campaigns are a key part to our marketing. Campaign content is both generic and reactive content. However, we always suggest that campaign content is planned ahead to make sure you don't miss out on any opportunities for your campaign. Your campaign would be standalone content from your reactive and generic content, and consistent with your branding different enough to make it stand out.

Making sure that you share reactive content regularly is important. If you just use generic content that is all scheduled and has no real-life business interaction or highlights, this can become 'same-y' to your audience. Your audience will tend to engage more with your reactive content and then ultimately will see more of your generic content as a result of this.

For example: It may be a team member's birthday, or a team member has taken part in a fundraising charity event. By posting this content, you will gather engagement and interaction which will give your generic content a boost in your audience's feeds; they will have shown they want to see more of your content in general, by engaging with the reactive content.

Tool Time: Crafting Content

The Creative Kit

When seeing all the amazing content being created and shared in our feeds, we start to wonder how we could create similar content without some of the advanced skills and tools that graphic designers and bigger brands may have.

Therefore, I would like to share a couple of user-friendly tools that you can utilise and don't need to have the full-on designer skills to operate.

The tools I share have some really good features and templates with which you can create some good quality branded images, videos, and content.

The first one I would like to introduce (and I am sure many of you have used) is Canva.com.

Canva is a graphic design tool which has 1000's of templates for you to create branded images, videos, lead magnets, website design banners, and much more. It's a drag and drop tool with lots of different elements such as icons, photos, and video stock that you can also use. This is a tool that I highly recommend for all beginners and people in marketing/social media to assist with your content creation.

Grammarly is another tool I would recommend. Lots of people have concerns about creating content and worrying about their spelling and grammar. This causes them to procrastinate and not post at all. Grammarly can be downloaded onto your laptop or desktop and will work on most applications including Canva, Social Media Management Tools and your Word documents. It will check for spelling and grammar errors enabling you to edit and amend before scheduling and posting.

These are just two of the many tools you can use when creating your content. I will list a few more in the resources chapter at the end of this book.

Your Next Move: Ready to Create Some Content?

It's now your turn! I have provided you with a lot of content here, enough for you to start creating the content for your lead magnet and the other services and products you would like to focus on.

So, pick a topic that your lead magnet covers, identify a related pain point, and create your first post! And remember, every piece of content is an opportunity to connect, help, and engage! But most importantly to start building your list.

If you would like to take it one step further, start planning your next 30 days!

"When you plan your content to maintain consistency, you have room for new content opportunities."

Chapter Six

Building Your List

Growing Your Digital Rolodex with Social Media

You will probably start seeing things come together. From identifying the pains and challenges of your target audience, to creating a lead magnet to give them a solution, to creating content that will resonate and get them engaged.

Now it's time to use that lead magnet to build your list, or sometimes I will call it building a raving fan base!

The Power of the List: Why Emails Still Matter

Many people still say to me, "Isn't building an email list a thing of the past? Emails don't work anymore."

Well... let me share something with you. I would say around four years ago when we were in the pandemic, Facebook and Instagram experienced a technical blackout. No one could access Facebook, they couldn't post, get to their messages, or communicate with their audience. For many businesses this is the only method of communication they have. It's the only platform where they can access their audience. So, when this blackout happened, I had many people getting in touch with me saying, "What am I going to do? This is my livelihood and the only way I can sell my products or services."

Many of these businesses have no website, no email list and won't have their existing customers noted down in a CRM (customer relationship management system).

This is one of the reasons why it's so important to build your email list. To make sure you have a way to get in touch with your customers. Many of those businesses that experienced that blackout have become customers of mine and they are all now successfully building their list of existing and potential customers.

We can spend so much time and resources on having conversations and building our audiences online, but remember, your audience is on a platform where there are so many profiles being hacked, taken over and being lost. This is why it's important to have an independent email list of your audience to make sure that this is never lost.

Social media is only one part of your marketing mix. Email marketing is also part of your marketing mix and should be used in alongside your social media to communicate with your existing and potential customers.

Beyond the Inbox

With social media being a key communication tool in our everyday lives offering quick, snappy information in short snippets, it also brings the challenges of ever-changing algorithms, the noise of too much information, and the volatility of the platforms.

Email has been a constant tool in the digital world over the years. It has been a reliable tool for professional and marketing communications.

Unlike the short-term presence of social media interactions, email presents an opportunity for personalised and targeted engagement. It empowers businesses and individuals to create content and messages that resonate with specific segments of their audience, creating stronger connections.

Businesses have complete control over their email marketing emails and communications, setting the tool apart from the ever-changing social media platforms algorithms which can affect the visibility of their content and potentially profile hacking and takeovers.

Trusty and Tangible

Your email list is built on permission-based engagement. People who have subscribed to your email list have chosen to share their contact information and, in doing so, have given you their permission to communicate with them. They have an interest in what you have to offer, forming an authentic and willing connection between you both.

An email allows a more personable communication. The emails you send will land in your audience's inbox, providing a one-on-one channel where you can address your subscribers by their names, making it more personalised. This direct line of communication provides a real connection, setting it apart from the more public social media interactions.

Having an email list allows you to develop and nurture long-term relationships over time with your audience. You can consistently send emails that provide value, share updates, and build trust. This will result in building know, like and trust relationships and create genuine connections that are interested in what you have to offer.

An email list allows you the ability to segment your list into different audience interests and demographics. This means you can create relevant emails and target your audience with content that resonates with them, increasing the engagement and relevance to them.

Over the years we have found that our audience members are able to communicate via email because they feel that they can have a private and secure conversation. This has increased the trust amongst our subscribers, and they have felt comfortable sharing their personal information this way.

An email list offers a unique and authentic way to build and nurture connections with your audience. It's a platform where you can engage with subscribers on a personal level, provide value, and achieve your business goals, while maintaining control and ownership of your audience.

Social Media Synergy: Boosting Your List Building

You're probably thinking… "Ok enough of the blurb about email marketing, let me start building my list and help me with some strategies!" Firstly though, I would like to share with you how social media and email marketing work hand in hand to not only help increase the reach of your message, but most importantly nurture your audience and convert them into clients.

The Dynamic Duo

Social media and email marketing can complement each other to expand your audience reach effectively. Social media platforms are great for engaging and attracting new followers, while email marketing allows you to nurture those connections, provide tailored content, and drive conversions.

Together, they create a powerful synergy for building and increasing your brand's reach and engagement.

From Scroll to Subscribe

There are so many strategies you can use to transition your social media followers into email subscribers, I could write a book about them alone!

I would like to share a few with you:

Create engaging content: Share exclusive, valuable content on social media, with teasers and snippets that encourage followers to join your email list for more in depth information or resources.

Competitions and Giveaways: Host competitions or giveaways on social media, asking participants to subscribe to your email list for a chance to win. The only downside to this is that you may attract an audience that may not be your ideal target audience.

Lead Magnets: This is one of the strategies we are going to use to build your email list! Promote lead magnets like eBooks, webinars, or downloadable resources via social media, directing your interested target audience to subscribe and access these valuable materials.

Exclusive Offers, Discounts or Early Bird Tickets: Provide special discounts, promotions, or early access to products/services exclusively to your email subscribers, encouraging social media followers to join your list.

Engagement and Interaction: Actively engage with your social media audience by responding to comments, questions, and messages. When responding to messages if you feel that your lead magnet will provide them with more in depth information and be a useful resource, send them a link to subscribe and access. This provides them with valuable information that they will be grateful for. This will build relationships and increase trust, making them more likely to subscribe.

Calls to Action: Always include clear and compelling calls-to-action (CTAs) in your social media posts and profiles, directing followers to subscribe to your email list for updates or special offers.

Work with Influencers and Partners: Partner with influencers or businesses that complement your services or products on social media. Working together to promote each other's email lists will help you expand your reach to new audiences that will become part of your overall target audience.

Consistency: Always maintain a consistent posting schedule on social media and regular email communication with your audience to keep followers engaged and encourage them to stay subscribed.

There are so many more strategies I could add, but these will get your started, and on your journey to building your list and growing your customer base.

As this chapter has been about creating a lead magnet, I would focus on sharing your lead magnet out on social media with the above strategies to start building your list.

Showcasing Your Lead Magnet: The 30-Day Blitz

Daily Dose

To get you started with the lead magnet strategy, I have put together a detailed 30-day calendar that offers a specific task each day to promote your lead magnet across the various social media platforms. Some of these may not be relevant for your target audience; if you come across a day that is not relevant, repeat a different day's set task.

Mix and Match

Every day on the 30-day calendar there is a fresh and engaging promotional tactic; you could use the calendar over and over again. You could even add your own personal touch or add your own tactics to vary the tasks.

As you will see, not every task will mean that you are posting to your feed, so you wouldn't be bombarding your audience with your lead magnet promotion over and over again.

The 30-Day Challenge: How Many New Subscribers Can You Attract?

Now you have learned the importance of email marketing and building your email list, it's now time for you to start putting the strategies into action and to attract your ideal audience.

Setting the Bar

I would like you to set a target of how many new subscribers you would like to achieve in the next month. When my new mentees ask me what is realistic, I say start with your first 100 subscribers, then 500, then 1000!

It's so important to keep your target goal realistic, remember the SMART goals we spoke about in the first chapter of this book. If you don't set a realistic goal, then you will likely set out with all good intentions to achieve your goal and then when it feels impossible you will lose momentum and give up.

So, start with your first 100 subscribers! Your first 100 raving fans :-)

Track and Triumph

It's so important to make sure you are monitoring the growth of your email list. This can involve using various tools and techniques to see what strategies are working best for you and that you are staying on track with your target.

Most email marketing platforms will provide an analytics feature which will share insights on how your list is growing, what content is attracting new subscribers to your list and how engaged they are with your emails. These metrics will enable you to tweak your strategies as needed to keep on track.

By regularly monitoring and tweaking your strategies, this can lead to your campaigns being more successful and therefore enable you to allocate more resources and budget to increase your efforts and success. Whilst monitoring, if your strategies are performing as well as they should then you can replace and tweak them without wasting too much time and resources on them.

I always advise my mentees to have milestones when building their email lists. Celebrate your milestone wins and successes. It's a great achievement to build your list; your subscribers are people who have expressed an interest in your brand and content! Acknowledge their value and make them feel welcome in your community; this can lead to higher engagement and loyalty in the long run. I will share some tactics on this in the next chapter.

Using tools to monitor progress, adapting your strategies based on insights, and celebrating new subscribers (or should I say raving fans!) to your email list are important to building and maintaining a healthy and engaged subscriber list.

Your Next Move: Ready to Grow Your List?

It's now your time to take action! With the 30-day lead magnet calendar available, I would love to set you the challenge of achieving your first 100 subscribers over the next month! Your first 100 warm leads.

I would love you to jump right in, stay consistent with the actions, and start growing your email list.

Remember every new subscriber is a sign of approval, a sign that you're on the right track and a sign that someone is interested in your content and brand. You have a solution for their pain and challenge, and this subscriber is a potential customer.

"Build an email list of raving fans who want to listen, engage and take action!"

Chapter Seven

Nurturing Your Email List with Care

Beyond the 'Hello'

When you start to build your list of interested prospects, you will have a sense of satisfaction. I love that feeling, it makes you realise that the solution you have been working on and the sweat and tears that have gone into it is exactly what your target audience need.

Your audience need the solution that your lead magnet is offering. Therefore, you can start to really push your lead magnet to build that email list of potential warm leads.

However, don't stop at just sending them the lead magnet! Whilst this can provide them with a solution, you have given them 'what' they need to do within this solution, not the 'how' they do it; and that is what they will be looking for help with next! So, if you stop at the lead magnet and don't follow up the communication with them, they could look elsewhere, for the product or service that you haven't offered.

I remember my mentor saying to me, "If you don't offer your services or products, when you understand the pains and challenges of your audience, then you are doing them a disservice. They will go elsewhere."

This is why it's so important to keep the communication between you and the subscribers to your email list, consistent, after that initial subscription.

Building Bridges

Being consistent in your email communications with your audience can strengthen the relationship but most importantly it will nurture your audience, building a 'know, like and trust' relationship with them.

I have so many clients and mentees say to me, "I can't email too often or I'll bombard them, they will get annoyed and unsubscribe." I normally reply, "If they unsubscribe then it's either not the right time for them to explore your solutions or knowledge topic, or they are no longer interested." I would rather people unsubscribe from my list when they are no longer interested, so it keeps my list fresh and the analytics accurate.

Whilst we are on this subject, I would love to address it properly, as so many people get upset, worry, and become uptight about people unsubscribing from their list. It's ok for this to happen, it just means that person no longer requires that knowledge or information anymore. Remember it's not personal. Move on and work on continuing to build the list of people who are interested to learn more and work with you.

Having a consistent email marketing plan of communications allows you to regularly keep in your audience's mind, reminds them of what you do, your credibility, and most importantly if they require your help, they will reach out to you at that time.

Know, Like, Trust: The Golden Trio of Email Marketing

The Friendly Nudge

When creating your emails, it's key to make sure that they have that personal and genuine feel to them. This enables your audience to get to know you better, and to establish that know, like and trust relationship.

There are many ways you can create a personal and genuine feel in your emails, and I am going to share a few of those ways with you.

Know your audience: By really knowing your audience's pains and challenges, this allows you to create emails that makes the reader feel you understand them fully. You can create content that resonates with them, and this will start to create that trust element. You can start to address their specific needs to further demonstrate that you really understand them.

Using personalisation: A feature that most email marketing software allows you to use is 'merge tags'. This enables your email to integrate the first name (or anything else you wish to add) into the email. This makes it more personalised.

There are also other personalisation features within email marketing softwares that allow you to segment your audience into different interests, behaviours, and demographics, enabling you to share relevant content, making it more relatable and relevant to your audience. This will create a feeling of being understood and being valued.

Tell your story: One of the ways in which I have built 'know, like and trust' with my audience, is by sharing my story with my subscribers. This establishes trust with them as they can relate your journey to their own journey and shows them why you do what you do. It also shares your credibility and that you're also human! I often share behind the scenes of what I'm doing which again makes my emails feel genuine and relatable.

Engage in two-way communication: Write your emails as though you are talking one to one with the subscriber. Ask them questions and give them the opportunity to respond to your email, or share their views, opinions, or questions online with you. This really creates a sense of community but also demonstrates that their opinion matters. However, please note, that it's ok asking for feedback and opinions, as long as you respond to them to show that you are listening and that you value their feedback and comments.

Lastly, **avoid over promotion** in your emails. You need to make sure that you have a good balance between the amount of promotional and valuable content information you send. Provide educational content, tips, or insights that benefit your subscribers. When they see that you're not just focused on selling, but also on providing value, it enhances the authenticity of your emails.

Building Credibility

One of the areas I will say that I have been successful in when building my business and personal brand over the last 13+ years is building my credibility and establishing 'know, like and trust' with my audience.

One of the ways in which I have done this is by always making sure that I have shared good valuable content. This could have been whilst on stage, on a podcast or webinar, delivering workshops and training, and when sending emails.

By sharing regular updates, trends, your stories and experiences, and most importantly valuable content that your audience can use and go and implement, is what will establish not only the like with your audience, but also for them to learn to trust you.

Once your audience trust you and you've nurtured them, it's then that you can convert your audience into buying customers and clients. And I will add... not just paying clients, introducers that refer people to you over and over again!

I have heard it said so many times, by so many so-called gurus, "Don't give too much away." But I truly believe that if you share some of your best content, then when people receive that great content they'll think, "Wow, they give this for free, what is it like when you pay them!" This puts you in a great position as you have established trust with them, and they'll be keen to work with you in the future on your paid services or products.

Another way you can build credibility is by sharing testimonials, behind the scenes, case studies, and most importantly results of how you have helped people.

Once upon a time, I was someone who had just left my role as an IFA/ Mortgage Broker and become a Social Media Consultant working from my front bedroom! I was lost as to how to build my profile; how would I build my credibility? I put myself out there, I spoke at every networking event I could, I connected with lots of event organisers, I exhausted my connection list by reaching out and asking to be connected, I did everything I could to get my name out there. I knew I'd been successful when one day I heard, "No Zoe, I can't have you speaking at our event as you have exhausted all the events in Kent!" I then realised that the hard work I'd put in to get my name out there in my area had paid off. The results were a reflection of my hard work.

I didn't stop there... my next goal was international status haha! I had always wanted to speak on international stages, and that is exactly what I did. I can proudly say that I have spoken in over 14 countries across the world. This is for another book.

Anyway, using all this credibility which has many stories behind it, is a great way to establish the 'know, like, and trust' with your audience in your emails. Be authentic and share your experiences. Allow your audience to feel that you understand them and can relate to their needs.

Your Email Blueprint: A Peek into the Sequence

The Journey

When working with my clients and mentees, I walk them through the journey of their first email sequence following from the lead magnet download.

When creating the sequence, you need to think about the customer journey; what would you like the subscriber to learn, or know, and then nurture them to eventually buy. I always suggest thinking about a low-cost product or service to introduce them to initially or getting them to book onto a discovery call with you. Both of these strategies work well: however, you just can't go and introduce this in the first email they receive from you. You need to nurture them first before upselling.

I always suggest that after every 3rd to 4th content or informational email you send a promotional email.

I have a basic flow chart and example email templates that you can download for your first email sequence. If you visit the website at the bottom of this page, you can download these templates for FREE!

Before you go and do this though, I would like to share a massive tip with you. One of the emails in the sequence that I have amazing success with is the email immediately sent after my lead magnet is downloaded with a delay of 4 hours. It is created to look like a personalised email from me, with no branding, and signed off by me.

This email basically just says, "Hi there, did you receive your 'XYZ' download ok? I just wanted to check, as I know sometimes emails get lost in our junk folders!"

You will not believe the number of emails I receive back from this that start a conversation with a warm prospect. Normally I get back, "Yes, all received and can't wait to read." I will then reply and say, "Great, any questions let me know." This gives me the opportunity to follow up with this person, start a phone call conversation, and nurture the relationship further.

If you already have a sequence, add this in! Give it a try and let me know the outcome.

Grab and Go

As I mentioned earlier, I would love you to start implementing your very own email sequence following the download of your lead magnet. So... I have created some ready-to-use templates to kick start your own email marketing campaign.

These are available to download from the below website. Remember make them personalised and specific to your brand, tone of voice, and topic.

Here is a sneak peek into the sequence:

I am going to share with you the six-part email sequence that we have used, tweaked, and defined over the years.

You will see the email sequence structure from the image, but I am also going to explain each email in a little more detail here:

Email One: Lead Magnet
(Sent immediately when someone subscribes)

This is the email that will automatically be sent to your new subscriber when they subscribe to your email list along with your lead magnet attached. Most software platforms have the feature 'automation' where this can be set up; this is connected to your opt-in form that you use on your landing page to capture your subscribers. The automation will detect a new subscriber and will then put that subscriber into this automated sequence.

Email Two: Personal Email
(Sent 4 hours after your first email and lead magnet, but also within the hours your audience would be active on email)

I recommend sending this second email around 4 hours after your first email and lead magnet. I also recommend that it has no branding on and looks like a personal email that you have sent to your subscriber and

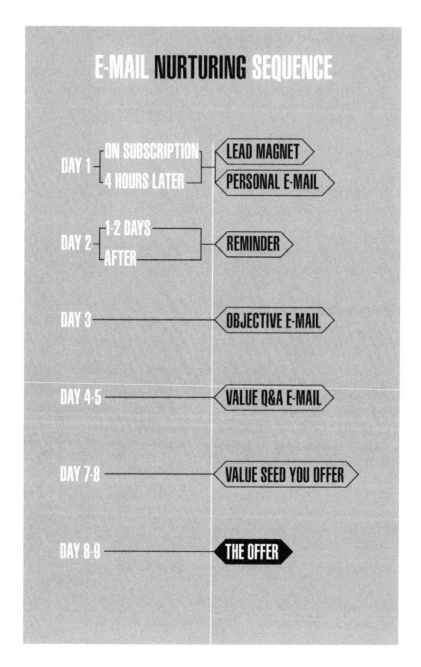

E-MAIL NURTURING SEQUENCE

DAY 1 — ON SUBSCRIPTION — LEAD MAGNET
4 HOURS LATER — PERSONAL E-MAIL

DAY 2 — 1-2 DAYS AFTER — REMINDER

DAY 3 — OBJECTIVE E-MAIL

DAY 4-5 — VALUE Q&A E-MAIL

DAY 7-8 — VALUE SEED YOU OFFER

DAY 8-9 — THE OFFER

written in real time (not that you have, but that's the perception). This email will ask your subscriber if they received your lead magnet successfully and to make sure it hasn't ended up in their junk folder. I will say, this email generates a lot of conversations with my subscribers, many of which have resulted in jumping on a call, consultation, and further conversions. Definitely not one to miss!

Email Three: Reminder
(Send 1-2 days after your Personal email)

When sending email three, I think about a topic or subject area within the lead magnet that I can highlight. This would then be created into a tip or conversation point in the email highlighting and revisiting the lead magnet. I would position this email as a 'reminder' about the lead magnet and how it would add value and benefit them, but also a content rich email which gives more additional content that they can utilise and take action on.

Email Four: Objections
(Send 2 days after your Reminder)

This email focuses on your subscribers' pains and challenges. You can remind them of the benefit of the lead magnet and highlight a pain or challenge that they would relate to and reinforce how the lead magnet would help them overcome this.

You can do this by sharing a case study, testimonial, personal story, or a FAQ.

Email Five: Value Q & A
(Send 2-3 days after your Objections email)

Your fifth email is about addressing some of the key questions your target audience ask but also adding valuable content that they will find useful. Think of 2-3 questions your audience would have around the topic discussed in your lead magnet and share the answers to those questions. You can add pictures, video clips and examples to demonstrate value and interest for this email.

Email Six : Value Seed Your Offer
(Send 3 days after your Value Q & A email)

In this email I recommend you provide more content, value, and information. Make sure it's inspirational and informative. You can also seed your offer in this email as well. What do I mean by 'seed'? Seed/seeding is when you mention about a service, product, programme, course, etc subtly in conversation, but not a pitch. Tease them and say that you will be sharing more about it soon! You're giving the 'what' in the email and making them shout, "But how?" and the 'how' is your solution; your product or service that is going to help them with that.

And that's the sequence...
I can hear you saying, "Hang on, what about the offer email :) ?!"

Email Seven: The Offer
(Send 1-2 days after your, Value Seed Your Offer email)

In this email you are going to share your offer. This is a promotional email. You have shared 3-4 emails with good content, that are informative and full of value. Now it's time to share your offer and start monetising your list.

As mentioned though, not every email after email seven should be promotional. I then recommending following the sequence again!

Head on over to the website to download the templates of the email nurturing sequence. Let me know how you get on.

Your Next Move: Ready to Nurture Those Subscribers?

Now that you are all set with the ready-to-use templates and my insights above, it's now time to create your own nurturing email sequence for your lead magnet or campaign.

Start with one email and focus on building a genuine connection with your subscriber. Keep the balance between promotional, and valuable or informative emails. Remember, every email is an opportunity to deepen the relationship, so make sure each one counts.

"Serve your audience genuinely, be their solution, and they'll choose you, every time, over any competitor."

Chapter Eight

The Two-Way Street: Why Engagement Isn't Just About Broadcasting

Beyond the Post

Social media isn't just about putting content out there, it's also about interacting and engaging with your audience.

This topic is something that I am passionate about as there are still so many people who use social media as merely a broadcasting tool. I like to always ask the following question: "Are you a broadcaster or are you an engager?"

A broadcaster is someone who uses a social media management tool or the scheduling feature within the platforms to just schedule posts. They will allow the posts to go out and then leave their social media activities there. Normally, they won't actually go into the social media platforms to check on their post engagement, or engage with their target audience in groups, other relevant pages, or within their inbox messages.

An engager is someone who also uses a social media management tool or the scheduling feature within the platforms to schedule posts. But they will also post reactive content from behind the scenes, on the day news, and interactive content. They will also take time to go into the actual social media platforms and engage with their audience. Comment on posts, go into groups, start conversations, and respond to inbox messages.

Which one are you? A broadcaster or an engager?

To have impact and get results from your social media activities you need to be an engager. It is crucial that you are not just broadcasting and speaking at your audience! This approach will mean a short-term journey for you on social media and you won't benefit from the results that you could achieve if you were actively engaging with your audience.

Community Over Crowds

Engaging with your audience, doesn't necessarily mean having thousands of followers and likes on your profiles. There was a time when follower numbers did matter, but that was until the algorithms came into place on the different platforms.

An algorithm is a rule /calculation that has been put behind the feeds and determines who sees your post on their social media feed. It determines how far your post will reach and how long it will stay in the feed. The more reach, potentially the more engagement (depends on good engaging content), the longer it stays on the feed, and the more people who will see it.

Now, with post algorithms, it's not about numbers. Followers and likes are very much vanity metrics. I always say, "Quality over Quantity."

Social media is all about building a strong community of people that engage, follow, and take action on your posts.

Why not a big audience? You could have a massive audience but only an average of 0.10% of them will see your posts and some of those people may not be interested in what you do.

Therefore, I would rather you- my mentees and clients - had a smaller following but with a strong level of interest, sense of community, and engagement.

Followers/Likes are easy to obtain, and there is still a large amount of people who will buy followers for vanity metrics on their page. Also, I have had a lot of people come to me (especially influencers) to help them monetise their followers. Some of them will have a large following, but with no engagement and therefore not monetising their activities.

Building a community is gold! And as I mention, in 'Zoe' words, "build a raving fan base."

Starting Conversations: The Art of the Nudge

The Gentle Prompt

The gentle prompt is something that I have often explained, and used, as part of the social media etiquette that I share with my mentees.

You will probably have experienced one of those pushy, salesy, cringy messages that try to sell to you as soon as you connect, or someone selling who bombards your business page post with a link and sales messages because you've had lots of engagement on it!

I tell people, that's just like going up to someone's stand at an exhibition and pinning your business card to that person's pop-up banner! Don't do it, it's bad social media etiquette.

The key to engagement is providing good value, answering the comments and questions from your community and when appropriate, directing them to your lead magnet, resources, or sending them to your inbox to private message you and continue the conversation. This is when you can start the warm lead to conversion process.

It's all about building a rapport, a 'know, like, and trust' factor with your audience, and then initiating the conversation with a gentle prompt, rather than coming off as pushy or salesy... or even cringy!

Lead Magnet Magic

I remember a time when I was giving so much away for free without being able to follow up with my connections or followers. I would provide the information requested via a comment, inbox or a webinar without collecting any contact information!

This is when my lead magnet provided the magic! It was a win, win for both myself, and my raving fans. I provided the knowledge, and in exchange they shared their contact information; I could then follow up with the 'gentle prompt'.
Most recently I had a business owner come to me and say she was having so many conversations online, there was so much engagement, but she had no clients, and no conversions.

When I looked at her engagement, it was great, but she was repeatedly sharing the same type of information and knowledge over and over again.

I then suggested to her about creating a lead magnet, a guide to provide to her 'raving fans' when they asked the question or engaged in conversation around the topics included in the guide, and also to direct her fans to more information that they could find useful.

When I shared with her the purpose of this, she was at first hesitant, I explained to her that her fans will find this more valuable (WHY?), they will encourage other people to read your guide, but most importantly, you will build an email list that you can follow up and nurture to conversion.

After a few months training and putting her lead magnet out LIVE, she was over the moon! She was seamlessly guiding her conversations, questions and engagement towards her free lead magnet and started turning the conversations into conversions.

Your Engagement Compass: The FREE Engagement Grid Checklist

Stay on Track

To make it easier for you I have put together an engagement grid checklist. This checklist will take you through step by step the daily engagement actions that I recommend for your social media activities.

It will ensure that you are engaging effectively and consistently.

Remember, only engage on the platforms where your audience are most active, and keep to the correct social media etiquette, making sure you don't alienate your audience and put them off.

It's all about building… wait for it… 'a raving fan base.'

You can access and download the engagement grid checklist for FREE by visiting the website shared below.

Daily Dose

Lots of people set tasks in their 'to do' list to engage daily. However, I know when you are a small business, you are trying to wear so many different hats. It can become a full-time job or more, to try and get everything done in the hours you have, working on your business.

Therefore, I always tell people to engage every other day, or at a push every third day, to put less pressure on yourself, but remember it's vital that you engage on your social media profiles.

If you can engage every other day for at least 15-20 minutes, this will be sufficient for you to start getting effective results from your social media activities.

Regular engagement is a key element of your social media activities and getting results.

You can use the engagement grid checklist as your daily, bi-daily guide!

20 Minutes to Triumph: The Daily Engagement Ritual

Algorithm Allies

As mentioned earlier, the social media platforms want you to engage with your audience. Social media is about engaging and making your audience feel part of a community. And this is why I asked you the question earlier, are you a broadcaster or an engager?

Social media is a two-way communication channel, where we share, contribute, communicate, educate, and create content that resonates and engages our audience. It's no longer the same broadcasting tool, where we could get away with constant promotional messages when the algorithms didn't exist, knowing that everyone would see our posts. It was too easy!

Now, it's about not beating the algorithms, but working with the algorithms and keeping up with the changes. It's about understanding what the platforms would like us to do, but most importantly ensuring that we are making a safe, engaging, happy environment for our audiences. Engagement is key to our potential reach on the platforms. The more we engage with our audience, then more our audience will engage back and therefore the more our posts will be shown to more people and stay longer on the feed!

By regularly engaging with your audience, you can make the algorithms your best friend.

Quality Over Quantity

It's not about how long you engage for, it's how meaningful you are, and how you are contributing to your community. It's all about adding value, conversation, and contribution.

Many of my mentees would ask me, how to make their 20 minutes really count. I provide them with the following advice that can help with their engagement activity.

Start Conversations - A great way to start a two-way communication with your audience is when they comment on your posts, you reply and ask a question. Get them to interact and start a conversation with them from there. You can then move this conversation into your inbox to follow up or get them on a call. Also, using conversation is a good way to get your posts in front of more people. As your post gains interest, it will be shown to more people because of the level of interest and audience engagement it is receiving.

Contribute - Check in the groups that you belong to on Facebook and LinkedIn and contribute to any conversations that are going on in those groups or that your target audience are engaging with or posting to. Remember though, don't spam the feed of conversation as this is not good etiquette. It's about contributing good valuable information, sharing resources and pointing your audience in the right direction. You can build your credibility and influence by contributing your opinion, knowledge, advice, and guidance.

Another tactic is to search for relevant hashtags on LinkedIn, Facebook, X and Instagram, and joining the conversations, or commenting on the posts with your expertise.

Add Value - If you can't find any discussions, can't contribute, or start a conversation, how about adding a valuable post in a group or on your feed? Ask an open question and get people commenting on your post to start that conversation. It's important that we share good valuable content; remember… quality content over quantity.

Respond - Make sure that you're getting back to your audience's comments and inbox messages in a timely manner. You don't want any enquiries or opportunities to go cold due to you leaving it 3-4 days before getting back.

Even if you can't manage 15-20 minutes a day engaging, at least allow 5 minutes to double check your profiles for any immediate actions required on new enquiries, or comments that are time sensitive. Then, allow time later that day to get back to the less urgent comments, making sure these are responded to. Why, might you ask? It's important to respond to your comments on your posts and your inbox messages because the algorithm will monitor this activity. It will be looking at your response time, but most crucially be looking at whether you respond to the comments to see if you are making your audience feel part of a community, and you're not just a broadcaster!

Allow for response time in your engagement activity. I have added this to the engagement grid checklist as one of your actions.

You will not believe the amount of people who have come to us and said that they don't get anything from social media! We then go into their inbox messages on Instagram and FB and check the 'secret' folder that many people miss called 'requests'. This is a folder where you may receive messages from someone you are not following but who has sent you a message; you may find quite a few enquiries if you haven't checked it regularly. Messages or enquiries from anyone you don't know yet or you haven't engaged with will land in this folder.

So… big tip, go and check your requests folder! You never know, you may have some warm enquiries in there.

The Bigger Picture: Engagement and Community Building

Algorithm Love

Start loving the algorithms rather than saying you want to beat them! We will never beat the algorithms, as no one except the platform managers know exactly what they are, and they change all the time. All we can do is make sure that we keep an eye on new updates, listen to what the platforms tell us they are looking for, and keep testing.

What we do know from years of testing, posting, and measuring at ZC Social Media, for the clients we work with, is that when you're consistent with your engagement on your social media activities, the more you will boost your standing with the social media algorithms, and the more visible you will become.

From Followers to Fans

I can honestly say that engagement is how you can transform your casual followers into loyal community members or 'raving fans' as I love to call them. A community who feels seen and valued.

Over the years, I have always made sure that even if I had a day when I wasn't posting, that I still took the time to engage with my audience. For my regular engagers, I would go and look at their posts on the different platforms and engage with those posts, get involved in conversations, and contribute. This would encourage them back to my profiles and get them engaging with my posts in return.

What you will also find, is that when your audience engages with one of your posts, the algorithm acknowledges that person's is interest in your content, and will show them more of your posts, until they no longer engage and then they will see less of you in their feed. Give it a try yourself; go and find someone on Facebook whose posts you haven't seen in a while, engage with one of their posts, and then go back to your feed. Guess what, I bet you see more of their content in your feed!

Your Next Move: Ready to Dive into Meaningful Conversations?

Let's get you engaging! And turning those of you who are just broadcasters into engagers.

With the engagement grid in hand and the above to guide you, it's now time to dive into the world of social media with a fresh focus on engagement.

I would love you all to start small, be genuine, and watch as your community grows and thrives. Remember, every interaction is an opportunity to connect, so make each one count!

"Don't be a broadcaster, be an engager!
Make your audience feel as though they are part of a community."

Chapter Nine

Why Advertise? The Boost You've Been Looking For

Beyond Organic

When you create content and you post it to your social media profiles, you are attracting viewers or customers to that post which is what we call 'organic reach'. It's the online equivalent of word-of-mouth; people find your content and offerings because of search results, direct links, or social shares. While it's a way to gain attention, it can often be slow and limited to who you are getting these posts in front of, especially if you have a smaller community or have just started out. In addition, the algorithms that the platforms have behind the feeds are determining who, when, and how many people see your posts.

It hasn't always been like this, before algorithms were introduced, when we posted to our feed, all of our connections would see our posts. However, Facebook and the other platforms wanted to find ways to make money, they decided that if they decreased their users reach, their users would want to increase their reach in order for more people to see their posts and messages; that's when they introduced the algorithms to reduce the reach and encourage people to use advertising. Advertising costs the users to use, and therefore this is where Facebook make their money. Advertising can make a significant difference when used in the right way and when you have a clear strategy.

Advertising is like adding a megaphone to your post and message. Instead of waiting for people to discover your content or offering organically, you can proactively showcase it to a targeted audience, ensuring it gets noticed quickly and by more people. So, while organic reach is valuable, when you want to increase your visibility or reach a wider audience, advertising becomes an invaluable tool for you to start using in your social media activities.

Targeted Reach

When you have created your valuable, problem solving, lead magnet, you will want it to be seen by those who will benefit from it the most; those who are experiencing that pain and challenge that your lead magnet solves. However, when posting organically to your profiles, whilst your existing audience will see it, your ultimate goal is to share your message with the wider audience, an audience that don't know who you are yet, or who would find your lead magnet useful. This is where advertising becomes invaluable in assisting you to spread your message to a wider target audience.

Advertising allows you to strategically place your lead magnet in front of the eyes of your target audience, even if they haven't met you yet. Instead of just creating your advert and hoping for the best, you can target specific demographics, interests, or behaviours. This is why it's so important to make sure that you have completed your target audience sheet to fully understand who your ideal customer is. It enables your content to reach people who are more likely to engage with it and who have the pain or challenge that your lead magnet is addressing. Plus, with the power of social media advertising features, you can choose the exact time and place for your lead magnet to appear, ensuring maximum relevance and impact in the areas you wish to push your lead magnet. By using social advertising, it will make sure that your lead magnet doesn't just get attention – it gets the right attention, right when it matters most for your target audience.

Strategies and Tactics: Making Your Ad Spend Count

Ad Essentials

Social adverts are available on most social media platforms including Facebook, Instagram, X, TikTok, Snapchat, Pinterest, LinkedIn, and YouTube.

Depending on who your target audience are, the social media platform you use to advertise on will change.

When creating adverts, I would love to share some key components of a successful ad. From compelling visuals to persuasive copy, here they are:

Compelling visuals: An image can say a thousand words, and the human brain can process can image faster than text. By adding a compelling image or even an informative, entertaining, or engaging video, you can instantly grab the attention of your target audience. It could be anything from a product shot, or an influencer, to user generated content, or an illustrative picture, but your image or video should resonate with your target audience and be relevant to your message; but most importantly be on brand!

Persuasive Copy: When people say that words matter, they really do matter. It's so important that your image or video attracts your audience, but more crucially that your copy then draws them in further to take action on your advert. Your copy should be clear, concise, and convey the main benefit or solution of your lead magnet, product, or service. You really need to resonate with your audience and speak directly to them, addressing the problem and challenge they may be experiencing.

Whilst we are talking about persuasive copy, I would love to share my 'perfect caption' formula. This is definitely something that will help you when writing future social media posts or adverts. If you follow this formula, you will find it easier to get across your message. It goes something like this:

Hook/Question
Blurb/Story
Call to Action

If you look at other adverts that similar businesses or brands are posting in your industry, you will see this similar structure to their copy. The hook or question does exactly as its name suggests and hooks your audience in. As they scroll, they will read the first line of the caption, whilst asking themselves the very same question, it resonates completely and draws them in! You then get the opportunity to explain in a paragraph or two, some informative content or a story about your lead magnet, product, or service in action. Share good valuable content here or share a story of someone you have helped. Then, lastly comes the call to action; what would you like your viewer to do? It's really important to only add one call to action, otherwise your viewer can get confused about what action to take.

Ultimately, when writing your copy, it's so important to make sure that your copy grabs your viewers' attention and that they relate to what you are saying, in order for them to take the action.

Clear Call-to-Action (CTA): As mentioned above, a clear call to action is key. What do you want your viewers to do after seeing your advert? Whether it's to 'Learn More', 'Shop Now', or 'Sign Up', a clear and direct CTA guides your viewer on to the next steps. It's the key action between just seeing an ad and taking action.

Consistency in Branding: It's really important to make sure that your advert follows your branding, tone of voice, and values. You don't want to be confusing your audience and making them question the advert because it doesn't relate to your existing brand and messaging. You need to make sure that your advert is going to be remembered and gains trust from your audience, and this can be achieved by making sure that it reflects your brand's identity. You can do this by making sure the use of colours, fonts, logos, and tone is consistent with your brand. An ad that looks and feels 'off-brand' can confuse viewers or make them sceptical.

Targeting & Placement: I've known clients and mentees who have come to me to ask for my help, and they have the best-looking adverts, but they haven't reached the right audience. I still today, have many conversations with potential clients who have created adverts and have got lots of people from different countries engaging with their advert, instead of from the place they wanted to target! They ultimately end up getting new followers and engagement from people on the platform who are not their target audience.

This is why it's so crucial to understand who your ideal customers are and where they spend their time. This ensures your advert appears in the right place, at the right time, and to the right people.

One big tip I would like to give, and especially if you have experienced the above scenario of irrelevant people liking, engaging, and interacting with your ad, I urge you to check the following option in your advert. When you select the audience for your advert, it asks you what locations you would like to target. Before you type in the locations, it gives you a couple of options of tick boxes along the lines of the following that you can choose from:

- People who live in this location

- People who lived in this location

- People who have recently been to this location

- People who have travelled through this location

When assessing my mentee or client's advertising efforts I normally find that they haven't changed or selected a relevant location option and realise that it's selected 'people who have travelled through this location'. This means it can show your advert to anyone who has travelled to that location from anywhere. This would then make your advert ineffective if you were intending to target an audience living in a local area. Please make sure you check this option on future advertising campaigns, it can really alter the results you are receiving and the audience that are engaging.

Engagement & Feedback: I know I have shared quite a bit about the importance of engagement in social media. With advertising it's also important to for your advert to be engaging and not just to be broadcasting your offer. Advertising is also about listening to your audience and finding out what their feedback and response is to your lead magnet, product, or service. Monitor when your advert is live and how your target audience are interacting with it. Are they clicking on it? Are they sharing or commenting? This feedback can provide valuable insights to tweak and improve your future adverts.
By implementing these key components, you can create an advert that not only catches the eye, but also resonates with the viewer and prompts action and engagement.

Lead Magnet Limelight

Let's look at some specific strategies to help your lead magnet stand out when creating adverts and attracts those clicks in a crowded ad space.

Please bear in mind these are the strategies we have used over the years and have had success when implementing.

Clear Value Proposition: Your lead magnet must offer a clear value. Whether it's an eBook, a webinar, or a discount, ensure that the primary benefit for your target audience is immediately understandable when they look at your advert. Your target audience should be able to answer the question, "What's in it for me?" and feel the need to take action on your advert.

High-Quality Design: We discussed earlier about making sure that your advert is on brand and in line with your company values. A professional looking design that is consistent with your branding will also give your lead magnet credibility. Think about investing in good visuals, readable fonts, design, and colours that may prompt emotions and that will align with your lead magnet and brand. There are so many different options when it comes to design. You can find a designer on tools like peopleperhour.com, fiverr.com or even use Canva.com to design yourself, especially if you have that creative flair.

Engaging Headlines: Your headlines are important to make sure they attract your target audience and grab them, in order for them to take action. Make sure they resonate, are concise, punchy, and create a sense of urgency.

Social Proof: When sharing your lead magnet advert you could include user generated content, content that shares testimonials, user stories, ratings, and case studies that showcase others using and finding value in your lead magnet, product, or service. Your audience will listen more to someone who has implemented and used your lead magnet, rather than from you as a brand. Your existing clients are much better advocates.

Clear and Actionable CTAs: Don't just tell your audience about your lead magnet, guide them on what to do next. Whether it's 'Download Now', 'Sign Up for Free', or 'Get Started'; make sure the call to action is clear for them not to miss it.

Test and Refine: A/B testing can be invaluable. By creating two versions of your advert with slight variations, you can see which one performs better and then optimise accordingly. It might be that you test two different images, different copy, or even a video versus an image. It's good to test, monitor, and tweak accordingly to see which works best with your audience.

Educational Content: This is one of our favourite strategies when getting your lead magnet out there. Before pushing your lead magnet, create informative content around its topic. Blog posts, videos, or posts can establish authority and make users more responsive when they see your adverts and posts that promote your lead magnet.

Remember, the advertising space can be very crowded with many businesses working to get their offers in front of their target audience, but with strategic thinking and a focus on value, your lead magnet can stand out and attract the clicks and attention it truly deserves.

Diving Deeper: Advanced Advertising Tips

Audience Precision

In Chapter two, I covered this extensively when thinking about who your target audience are, along with their demographics, interests, pains, and challenges. However, I wanted to share a few more tips on segmenting and targeting your audience for maximum impact when it comes to social advertising. Here are some key areas I share with my clients and mentees to go through when thinking about their audience before creating their campaigns or adverts:

Start Basic: First, think about the audience you would like to talk to. Are they from a certain age group? Do they live in a particular area or location? These basic demographics help in reaching a more specific audience.

What Do They Like?: Think about what they're interested in. They might love sports, gardening, or cooking. This helps you tailor your content and talk to them in ways that they can relate to.

Watch Their Actions: Look at how people react to what you offer. Do they engage with your page? Did they buy something once but not come back? Knowing this can help you figure out what to show them next.

Solve Their Problems: Think about the pains and challenges of your target audience and how you can help them. If you know what they're looking for, you can create the copy that will resonate with them.

Make it Personal: Once you know your audience, make sure you talk to them in ways that feel personal. If they feel you understand them, they're more likely to engage.

Check and Change: People's likes and habits change over time. We recommend that you revisit your target audience analysis every quarter and to research any new interests, behaviours, and demographics.

Think Local: If you're talking to people from your local area, try to include things that matter to them locally.

Remember, reaching the right people is all about understanding them and knowing your audience well. The more you get to know them, the better you can communicate and offer them things they need and love.

Budgeting Brilliance

One of the frequently asked questions I get about social advertising is how much should we budget per advert? How much should be put aside for ad spend?

There are many factors I share when considering your budget for advertising. I would like to share them with you now.

Define Your Goals: Decide what you want from your adverts. More email subscribers? More followers? Increased sales? Setting clear objectives can help guide your budget for your social advertising.

Research Platforms: Not all social platforms get the same results. Investigate where your target audience hangs out the most and prioritise these platforms for your social advertising efforts.

Diversify Spending: Don't put all your money into one platform or ad type. Spread your spending across different ads such as image ads, video ads, carousel ads and different platforms for better risk management. It's all about testing to see which platform performs best. You can then concentrate more on the platform where you are getting the best results.

Monitor Ad Performance: Regularly check how your ads are doing. Don't just put them live and then leave them. One of the most important tips I can give you is to set a date in your diary as to when your advert needs to be turned off, and also that you allocate time in your engagement exercise to monitor how your adverts are performing. All platforms that offer social advertising provide insights that you can monitor. Personally, I always tell my mentees and clients to download the 'Facebook Ads App' from Meta to monitor your adverts more easily. Use the data to see where your money's working best and what advert is performing better.

Adjust On-the-Go: Be ready to reallocate funds. If an ad isn't performing, consider reducing its budget and putting more into what's working.

Expert Insights: Occasionally, consult peers or experts. They might offer tips on getting more from your advertising budget. They will keep up to date with the latest trends and updates in the social advertising industry.

Social advertising is a big topic and is not an overnight tactic that you can learn. It takes time, practise, and experience to run successful campaigns. Being adaptable and regularly reviewing performance is key, it will ensure that you're getting the most from your advertising budget.

Learning from the Best: Industry Research with Facebook Ad Library

Ad Detective

It's time to be an Ad Detective! I recommend implementing this action regularly to see what others in your industry are up to! You can do this by using the Facebook Ad Library:

The Facebook Ad Library: Step by Step Guide

The Facebook Ad Library is a valuable tool for marketers looking to get insights on what competitors and others in the industry are doing.

Here's a beginner-friendly step-by-step guide:

1. **Access the Library**: Navigate to the Facebook Ad Library. You can easily find it by searching for 'Facebook Ad Library' on your preferred search engine or by visiting the direct link on Facebook.

2. **Search for a Business Page**: In the search bar, type the name of the organisation or brand you would like to research. As you type, suggestions will drop down. Click on the correct one.

3. **Filter Your Results**: Once on the page, you can filter results by:

   a. **Country:** View ads that are shown in specific regions.

   b. **Ad Status:** See active ads or those that have concluded.

4. **Dive Into Individual Ads**: Click on 'See Ad Details' for any advertisement to get more info. Here, you can view:

   a. The ad's creative content (image, video, text).

   b. Duration the ad has been running.

   c. The estimated range of ad spend and impressions (for political or issue ads).

5. **Explore Different Ad Types:** Some brands run multiple versions of an ad or different ads for various platforms (like Instagram or Facebook). Scroll through to see the different adverts they are running.

6. **Issues, Elections, and Politics Option:** If you're interested in ads about social issues, elections, or politics, there's a separate tab.

These ads have more detailed insights due to transparency requirements.

7. **Take Notes:** As you research, note down the strategies or ad creatives that stand out to you. Try to recognise whether you can see the 'perfect caption', remember hook, story, call to action! Consider what makes the ads engaging. Are they using video content? How's their ad copy?

8. **Regularly Revisit:** Advertising updates and trends change all the time. Regularly checking the Ad Library ensures you're up to date with the latest industry tactics.

Remember, while the Facebook Ad Library provides valuable insights, always ensure your ads are in line with your brand. It's great to be inspired by others in your industry and gain ideas, but your unique voice and value proposition are what will truly resonate with your audience.

Your Action Plan: Ready to Dive into the World of Social Advertising?

I have shared quite a few tips and tactics around the use of social media advertising, it's now time for you to create your first advert.

I would like you to start with your lead magnet, use the Facebook Ad Library for research, and experiment with different strategies. Remember, it's about making sure that you use the 'perfect caption', highlight the solution you are providing that helps with their pain or challenge.

Set yourself a target of how many people you would like to download your lead magnet in a specific time period. Monitor this goal. Measure your success.

Successful advertising is all in the testing, learning, and refining.

Whilst this chapter shares with you the 'what' about social advertising, you're probably wondering about the 'how'. We run regular sessions in the ZC Social Media Growth Academy that can take you step by step through planning, creating, monitoring, and measuring your social media adverts.

"Successful advertising is all in the testing, learning, and refining."

Chapter Ten

A Look Back: The Chapters of Beyond The Feed

From Start to Finish

Our journey with this book 'Beyond The Feed', started with the importance of social media goals in 'Dream Big, Start Smart'. It was here that we explored setting clear, aligned goals and objectives that become a crucial plan to tackle the overwhelming world of social media. I also shared the importance of not just dreaming big, but starting with smart goals, making sure that every step taken on social media aligns with your business ambitions.

Navigating further, we explored your audience in more depth in 'Your Target Audience'. I shared the tools of understanding your audience's pains and challenges and how they will assist you in creating compelling content. By understanding these key pains and challenges it enables you to create your 'Lead Magnet', this is where we highlighted the success gained from attracting warm leads and building a strong email list. With 'Nurturing Your List', we emphasised the importance of following up and engagement, ensuring every subscriber feels valued and connected.

We then moved on to 'Engagement'; looking at the two-way communication of social media interactions, and the importance of building strong communities as opposed to simply gaining more followers. This then set the relevance for 'Social Media Advertising', where we looked at the potential of targeted adverts, ensuring your message reaches the right audience at the right time.

Throughout 'Beyond The Feed', the main theme has been clear: Social media isn't just about broadcasting; it's about building authentic, meaningful connections. It's about understanding, engaging, and growing with your audience. And as we wrap up with resources and insights about the me, the author, I hope you're equipped with not just knowledge, but the passion and drive to get results from your social media activities.

The Formula in Focus

The main purpose of 'Beyond The Feed' is to share a clear and simple plan: the **Social Media Success Formula**. Think of it as your step-by-step guide to get the most from your social media activities.

We started with **Goals**, setting clear aims for what you would like to achieve online. Next, we got to know your **Audience** – who they are and what they're looking for. With that in mind, we looked at the **Lead Magnet**, a way to grab their attention and keep them interested. Then, we talked about **Content**, or the stuff we share online to keep our audience engaged and coming back for more.

From there, we moved to **Building Your List**. This is all about gathering a group of people who are genuinely interested in what you have to say. With that list, we then explored **Engagement**, and the tactics of chatting with your audience and making them feel valued. **Nurturing Your List** was all about keeping that conversation going, making sure our audience knows we're here for them. And lastly, with **Social Advertising**, we looked at ways you can reach even more people and spread your message further to a wider audience.

All these steps come together to form a straightforward plan for connecting with people online, building genuine relationships, and getting results from your social media.

Beyond the Pages

Whilst this book offers many insights and strategies, it's value will be determined in what you do with this knowledge. It's one thing to read and acknowledge the steps along the way, but the results happen when you start to put these ideas into action.

Think of 'Beyond The Feed' as a conversation between me and you. I've shared my experiences and expertise, and now it's over to you to take the action. Take these lessons, tweak them to suit your social media journey. Remember, every page you've turned, every chapter you've explored, is one more step towards your social media success. So, don't just keep this knowledge noted in a notebook, or put it back on the shelf; write a plan, start implementing and experimenting, and watch as you start to see the results from your social media activities.

Accountability Matters

Consistency in social media is key. It's easy to start with a period of motivation, but the real challenge is keeping the momentum and the consistency. This is where I would recommend accountability. By setting clear goals and milestones for yourself, you then will not only have a good plan but also targets to measure your success.

It's also so important to remember that we are human and will experience ups and downs. Days when we don't have the motivation, or things in our personal lives that overtake and affect our online journey. That's ok, but remember always think of the bigger picture, and don't forget to celebrate the small wins. The small wins are important as well as they showcase our progress, commitment, and consistency. By celebrating each small step on our journey, we can get the all-important boost of motivation and demonstrate that we are staying focused on our goals. Share and celebrate small steps every day.

Also, think about connecting with someone who is also working on their own social media journey. Become accountability partners, where you keep each other on track, check in and keep each other motivated through times when most needed.

I've always had an accountability partner to keep me on track. A 30-minute meeting every week or every other week to recap on progress, goals, and challenges, enables you to clarify and share, but most importantly gives you the push you need to keep going forward.

Measure, Refine, Repeat

Whilst using these strategies, tactics, and taking action, it's important to make sure that you are always measuring the results. This enables you to refine your activities and go forward with what's working and stop doing what's not working.

I always suggest scheduling in your diary to check a 'weekly snapshot', especially if you are running a social media campaign such as a launch. Check what has worked that week and see how you can repurpose the content that has worked to go forward with your campaign. Most importantly, always create a monthly report of your social media analytics to fully analyse your activity and to refine and repeat the activities and content that have worked well.

A quote that I have love from **Henry Ford** and has had a big impact on anything that I do in my business is:

"If you always do what you've always done, you'll always get what you've always got."

It's so true, if we don't change or refine what's not working, we will also get the same results. That's why it's so important to measure what you're doing for your social media activities.

Your Next Steps: The Journey Continues

The Road Ahead

The world of social media is always changing. With new updates, trends and features all happening daily, it's important to stay updated but most importantly be ready to adapt your strategy and activities according to those changes.

However, don't get distracted by a shiny new platform that everyone is jumping on and exploring. Remember to research to see whether it would be relevant for your brand but most importantly, are your audience going to be hanging out there? If you feel it is appropriate, give it a three-month trial, then analyse whether it's something that you will continue to invest your time and resources in.

As I say to my mentees in our ZC Social Media Growth Academy on our monthly 'Trends and Updates' webinar, it's so important to make sure you have a reason as to why you're going to use a new feature or platform, and that it aligns with your goals and the bigger picture.

Revisit your strategy every 6 months, although with the fast-paced social media changes and updates, I recommend reviewing every 3 months if you can. You will be monitoring your analytics monthly and making sure they still align with your goals.

Parting Wisdom

In my final words of this book, I would love you to go for it! Take the plunge and take the action. One of the many things I would love to share is that I have always been someone to take massive action. Learn, take action, see the results. It can be so motivating when you start to see things come together.

Remember it doesn't happen overnight. Social media is a long-term activity. However, when you come across well and share your authenticity, share good valuable content, engage with your audience, and continue to keep on top of the latest trends and updates, you will start to reap the rewards of your social media actions.

Most importantly, if you are building your own personal brand 'Be You', establish a 'know, like and trust' relationship with your audience so that they become your raving fans! A community that will encourage you, be there for you, but most importantly, feel valued by you.

What are you waiting for...It is time to now take the action. I wish you every success on this journey.

"If you always do what you've always done, you'll always get what you've always got."

Henry Ford

(my favourite quote)

Chapter Eleven

Your Toolkit: Resources to Assist Your Social Media Journey

Links and Recommendations

Zoe Cairns and ZC Social Media

Zoe Cairns: http://www.zoecairns.com
ZC Social Media: http://www.zcsocialmedia.com
ZC Social Media Growth Academy: http://www.zcsocialmediaacademy.com
Social Media Planner: http://www.zcsocialmedia.com/social-media-success-planner

Chapter One:

Actionable worksheets, guides, checklists and resources can be found at http://www.beyondthefeed.com
My Mindset/Business Mentor: Ash Lawrence http://www.ashlawrence.co.uk
My Sales/Online Mentor: Tony Bianco https://www.linkedin.com/in/tonybianco/
Book Mentor: Karen Stanley https://www.mabelandstanleypublishing.com/

Chapter Three:

Target Audience Sheet: http://www.beyondthefeed.com

Audience pains, challenges, and questions: http://
www.answerthepublic.com
Key questions asked by your audience: http://www.google.com
Forum of questions: http://www.quora.com
Trending questions and video tutorials: http://www.youtube.com
Brainstorming whiteboard tool: http://www.jamboard.google.com
Creative ideas and suggestions: http://www.pinterest.com

Chapter Four:

Design tool: http://www.canva.com
Lead magnet hosting tool: http://www.attract.io
Automated webinar platform: http://www.easywebinar.com
Live webinars and online meetings: http://www.zoom.com
Hosting video content: http://www.youtube.com http://
www.vimeo.com
Quiz and scorecard marketing: https://danielpriestley.com/scorecard-marketing/
30-Day promotional calendar: http://www.beyondthefeed.com

Chapter Five:

Metricool Social Media Management Tool: http://www.metricool.com
Design tool: http://www.canva.com
Spelling and grammar tool: http://www.grammarly.com
Chat GPT for ideas and suggestions: https://chat.openai.com/

Chapter Six:

Email marketing software: http://www.mailchimp.com (Start here as it
gives you 500 contacts for FREE)

Automation and email marketing software: http://www.activecampaign.com and http://www.keap.com
Competitions and giveaways: https://kingsumo.com/
30- Day promotional calendar: http://www.beyondthefeed.com

Chapter Seven:

Email templates for nurturing sequence: http://www.beyondthefeed.com

Chapter Eight:

Free engagement grid checklist: http://www.beyondthefeed.com

Chapter Nine:

Facebook Ad Library: www.facebook.com/ads/library
ZC Social Media Growth Academy: http://www.zcsocialmediaacademy.com

Chapter Ten:

Accountability Group: http://www.zcsocialmediaacademy.com
Business/Mindset Accountability Group: http://www.ashlawrence.co.uk

One-Click Access:

To quickly find and access the checklists, guides, and workbooks you can visit http://www.beyondthefeed.com where all the resources will be accessible.

My Offerings: Tailored Tools and Training

Programmes And Training

I offer bespoke 1-2-1 training sessions tailored to your individual needs and level of expertise in social media. Whether you're a beginner or looking to upskill, I'll walk you through each step, ensuring a hands-on learning experience. For those who opt for our packages, there's the added benefit of WhatsApp support for any queries on the go. Additionally, I provide corporate training for internal comms and marketing teams, ensuring they stay updated with the latest trends and updates, even amidst their busy schedules.

For more information email: info@zcsocialmedia.com

The Social Media Planner

Introducing our Social Media Planner, a trusted planner for many of our mentees, clients, and professionals worldwide for the past seven years. This planner is more than just a diary; it's a comprehensive tool designed to streamline your social media strategy. With features like a 90-day planning section, dedicated spaces for jotting down key dates and events, and a measurement area to track your progress, it ensures you stay ahead of the curve. And for those seeking an extra edge, our VIP package offers monthly content planning sessions, guiding you every step of the way. Year after year, this planner has proven to be an invaluable asset in crafting a cohesive and effective social media presence.

http://www.zcsocialmedia.com/social-media-success-planner

Advanced Learning And Support

Agency Insights

Established in 2010, ZC Social Media has grown from its humble beginnings to become a trusted brand for a range of clients, from startups to well-known international organisations. Our agency is dedicated to elevating your social media activities, offering a range of services bespoke to your needs. Whether it's planning and creating impactful social media campaigns, managing your daily social media activities, delivering engaging talks on the power of social media, strategising advertising campaigns, or providing hands-on training and workshops, we've got you covered. With a decade of experience, ZC Social Media is here to provide the expertise and support you need to harness the power of social media for your business.

http://www.zcsocialmedia.com

Membership Magic

The ZC Social Media Growth Academy is a hub designed for business owners, entrepreneurs, and social media enthusiasts looking to elevate their social media skills and knowledge. Our academy is more than just a membership; it's a vibrant community where like-minded individuals come together to stay updated with the latest trends, plan their monthly content, and explore the new changes of social media.

What sets our academy apart is the collective spirit of accountability, ensuring everyone stays on track. Members gain exclusive access to a vast video library with over 300+ hours of content, an area of useful resources, and the opportunity to engage in 4-5 LIVE sessions every month with myself and our dedicated team. These sessions are interactive, allowing for questions and discussions.

And the best part? We've made continuous learning accessible with an affordable monthly subscription, ensuring everyone can benefit from it!

http://www.zcsocialmediaacademy.com

Your Next Steps: Ready To Level Up?

Beyond The Basics

If you're looking to learn more and take your social media journey to the next step, explore some of the advanced resources and training available above. It's a great way to build on what you've learned and refine your approach to social media.

Stay Connected

Come and join my communities on social media! I would love to stay connected and hear all about your social media journey after reading #BeyondTheFeed.
Connect with me on the different platforms here:

Facebook: https://www.facebook.com/ZoeCairnsUK
X (formerly known as twitter): https://twitter.com/zoe_cairns
LinkedIn: https://www.linkedin.com/in/zoecairns/
Instagram/Threads: https://www.instagram.com/zcairns/
TikTok: https://www.tiktok.com/@zoecairns
YouTube: https://www.youtube.com/@ZoeCairns
Email: zoe@zcsocialmedia.com
Web: http://www.zoecairns.com

Download the FREE
social media success resources here:

www.beyondthefeed.com

Behind the Pages: Meet Zoe Cairns

Where I'm From

Born in Chatham and raised in Rochester, Medway, I've always felt a strong connection to my hometown. My early days in mortgage brokering and financial advising unexpectedly led me to the world of social media. And, as they say, the rest is history.

My Work Life

I've been fortunate to work with a diverse range of businesses, from local startups to big names in the Fortune 500 list. My love for social media strategy has opened doors for

me, allowing me to share insights in over 14 countries across the world including Poland, India, and Malaysia. I've even had the unique experience of training a multi-million company in Madrid and speaking at a conference for NATO in Montenegro. It's been quite the ride!

A Bit of Media Here and There

You might have caught me on the telly a few times. I've chatted about social media on ITV's 'This Morning' and BBC World News. It's always a bit surreal but fun to share my knowledge and help others watching.

All About ZC Social Media

Around 13 years ago, I took the leap and started ZC Social Media. What began as a small idea in my front bedroom has grown into a reputable agency. We're not just about making social media plans; we're passionate about teaching and empowering others in this space.

A Little More About Me

When I'm not immersed in the digital world, I'm spending quality time with Gareth Cairns, my partner in both life and business adventures. We're proud parents to three playful huskies. Travel is another passion of mine, with memorable trips to places like Yellowstone, Alaska, and Finland. And when it's time to unwind, there's nothing like a good book or a catch-up with loved ones.

Printed in Great Britain
by Amazon

37753522R00076